经典的回声·ECHO OF CLASSICS

中国古代寓言选
ANCIENT CHINESE FABLES

杨宪益
戴乃迭　　等英译

Translated by
Yang Xianyi, Gladys Yang and Others

外文出版社
FOREIGN LANGUAGES PRESS

图书在版编目（CIP）数据

中国古代寓言选/杨宪益，戴乃迭英译.
－北京：外文出版社，2001．8
（经典的回声）
ISBN 7-119-02887-1
I. 中… II. ① 杨…② 戴… III. 英语－对照读物，

寓言－汉、英 IV. H319.4:I

中国版本图书馆 CIP 数据核字（2001）第 042720 号

外文出版社网址：
　http://www.flp.com.cn
外文出版社电子信箱：
　info@flp.com.cn
　sales@flp.com.cn

经典的回声（汉英对照）
中国古代寓言选

译　　者	杨宪益　戴乃迭	
责任编辑	杨春燕	
封面设计	席恒青	
印刷监制	蒋育勤	
出版发行	外文出版社	
社　　址	北京市百万庄大街 24 号	邮政编码　100037
电　　话	（010）68320579（总编室）	
	（010）68329514 / 68327211（推广发行部）	
印　　刷	三河市汇鑫印务有限公司	
经　　销	新华书店 / 外文书店	
开　　本	大 32 开	字　数　150 千字
印　　数	5001－8000 册	印　张　8.875
版　　次	2004 年 1 月第 1 版第 2 次印刷	
装　　别	平装	
书　　号	ISBN 7-119-02887-1 / I · 693（外）	
定　　价	12.00 元	

出 版 前 言

　　本社专事外文图书的编辑出版,几十年来用英文翻译出版了大量的中国文学作品和文化典籍,上自先秦,下迄现当代,力求全面而准确地反映中国文学及中国文化的基本面貌和灿烂成就。这些英译图书均取自相关领域著名的、权威的作品,英译则出自国内外译界名家。每本图书的编选、翻译过程均极其审慎严肃,精雕细琢,中文作品及相应的英译版本均堪称经典。

　　我们意识到,这些英译精品,不单有对外译介的意义,而且对国内英文学习者、爱好者及英译工作者,也是极有价值的读本。为此,我们对这些英译精品做了认真的遴选,编排成汉英对照的形式,陆续推出,以飨读者。

外文出版社

Publisher's Note

Foreign Languages Press is dedicated to the editing, translating and publishing of books in foreign languages. Over the past several decades it has published, in English, a great number of China's classics and records as well as literary works from the Qin down to modern times, in the aim to fully display the best part of the Chinese culture and its achievements. These books in the original are famous and authoritative in their respective fields, and their English translations are masterworks produced by notable translators both at home and abroad. Each book is carefully compiled and translated with minute precision. Consequently, the English versions as well as their Chinese originals may both be rated as classics.

It is generally considered that these English translations are not only significant for introducing China to the outside world but also useful reading materials for domestic English learners and translators. For this reason, we have carefully selected some of these books, and will publish them successively in Chinese-English bilingual form.

Foreign Languages Press

目　　录
CONTENTS

中国古代寓言选

ANCIENT CHINESE FABLES

愚公移山

　　太行、王屋二山,方七百里,高万仞。

　　北山愚公者,年且九十,面山而居。惩山北之塞出入之迁也,聚室而谋曰:"吾与汝毕力平险,指通豫南,达于汉阴,可乎?"杂然相许。

　　其妻献疑曰:"以君之力,曾不能损魁父之邱,如太行、王屋何!且焉置土石?"

　　杂曰:"投诸渤海之尾,隐土之北。"

　　遂率子孙,荷担者三夫,叩石垦壤。箕畚运于渤海之尾。邻人京氏之孀妻有遗男,始龀跳,往助之。寒暑易节,始一返焉。

　　河曲智叟笑而止之曰:"甚矣,汝之不

HOW THE FOOL MOVED MOUNTAINS

Taihang and Wangwu Mountains are some seven hundred *li* around, and hundreds of thousands of feet high.

North of these mountains lived an old man of nearly ninety, who was called the Fool. His house faced these mountains, and he found it very inconvenient to have to make a detour each time he went out and came back; so one day he summoned his family to discuss the matter.

"Suppose we work together to level the mountains?" he suggested. "Then we can open a road southward to the bank of the Han River."

To this they all agreed. Only his wife was dubious.

"You haven't the strength to level even a small hill," she objected. "How can you move these two mountains? Besides, where will you dump all the earth and rocks?"

"We'll dump them in the sea," was the reply.

Then the Fool set out with his son and grandson, the three of them carrying poles. They dug up stones and earth, and carried them in baskets to the sea. A neighbour of theirs named Jing was a widow with a son of seven or eight, and this boy went with them to help them. It took them several months to make one trip.

惠！以残年余力，曾不能毁山之一毛，其如土石何？"

北山愚公长息曰："汝心之固，固不可彻，曾不若孀妻弱子！虽我之死，有子存焉；子又生孙，孙又生子；子又有子，子又有孙；子子孙孙，无穷匮也。而山不加增。何苦而不平！"河曲智叟无以应。

—— 《列子》

A man living at the river bend, who was called the Wise Man, laughed at their efforts and did his best to stop them.

"Enough of this folly!" he cried. "How stupid this is! Old and weak as you are, you won't be able to remove even a fraction of the mountains. How can you dispose of so much earth and stones?"

The Fool heaved a long sigh.

"How dull and dense you are!" he said. "You haven't even the sense of the widow's young son. Though I shall die, I shall leave behind me my son, and my son's sons, and so on from generation to generation. Since these mountains can't grow any larger, why shoudn't we be able to level them?"

Then the Wise Man had nothing to say.

Lie Zi

失斧疑邻

　　人有亡铁者,意其邻之子。视其行步,
窃铁也;颜色,窃铁也;言语,窃铁也;动作
态度,无为而不窃铁也。

　　俄而扬其谷而得其铁。

　　他日,复见其邻人之子,动作态度,无
似窃铁者。

——《列子》

SUSPICION

A man who lost his axe suspected his neighbour's son of stealing it. He watched the way the lad walked— exactly like a thief. He watched the boy's expression—it was that of a thief. He watched the way he talked—just like a thief. In short, all his gestures and actions proclaimed him guilty of theft.

But later he found his axe himself when he went out to dig. And after that, when he saw his neighbour's son, all the lad's gestures and actions looked quite unlike those of a thief.

Lie Zi

歧路亡羊

　　杨子之邻人亡羊。即率其党,又请杨子之竖追之。

　　杨子曰:"嘻!亡一羊,何追者之众?"

　　邻人曰:"多歧路。"

　　既反。问:"获羊乎?"曰:"亡之矣。""曰:"奚亡之?"曰:"歧路之中又有歧焉。吾不知所之,所以反也。"

　　杨子戚然变容,不言者移时,不笑者竟日。

　　门人怪之,请曰:"羊,贱畜,又非夫子之有,而损言笑者何哉。"

　　杨子不答。门人不获所命。弟子孟孙阳出,以告心都子。

TOO MANY PATHS

One of Yang Zi's neighbours, who lost a sheep, sent all his men out to find it, and asked Yang Zi's servant to join in the search.

"What!" exclaimed Yang Zi. "Do you need all those men to find one sheep?"

"There are so many paths it may have taken," the neighbour explained. When his servant returned, Yang Zi asked him: "Well, did you find the sheep?"

He answered that they had not. Then Yang Zi asked how they had failed to find it.

"There are too many paths," replied the servant. "One path leads to another, and we didn't know which to take, so we had to come back."

At that Yang Zi looked very thoughtful. He was silent for a long time, and did not smile all day.

His pupils were surprised.

"A sheep is a trifle," they said, "and this wasn't even yours. Why should you stop talking and smiling?"

Yang Zi did not answer, and his pupils were puzzled. One of them, Mengsheng Yang, went out to describe what had happened to Xindou Zi.

心都子曰："大道以多歧亡羊,学者以多方丧生。学非本不同,非本不一,而末异若是。唯归同反一,为亡得丧。子长先生之门,习先生之道,而不达先生之况也,哀哉!"

————《列子》

"When there are too many paths," said Xindou Zi, "a man cannot find his sheep. When a student has too many interests, he fritters away his time. The source of all knowledge is one, but the branches of learning are many. Only by returning to the primal truth can a man avoid losing his way. You are Yang Zi's pupil and study from him, yet you seem to have failed completely to understand him."

Lie Zi

献 鸠

邯郸之民,以正月之旦献鸠于简子。
简子大悦,厚赏之。

客问其故。

简子曰:"正旦放生,示有恩也。"

客曰:"民知君之欲放之。竞而捕之,
死者众矣。君为欲生之,不若禁民勿捕。
捕而放之,恩遇不相补矣。"

简子曰:"然。"

—— 《列子》

PRESENTING DOVES

It was the custom in Handan to catch doves to present to the prince on New Year's Day, for this pleased him so much that he gave rich rewards. Someone asked the prince the reason for this custom.

"I free the doves at New Year to show my kindness, " he said.

"Since your subjects know you want doves to set free, they all set about catching them, " objected the other. "And the result is that many doves are killed. If you really want to save the doves, you had better forbid people to catch them. As things are, you catch them to free them, and your kindness cannot make up for the damage you do."

The prince agreed with him.

Lie zi

砍倒了梧桐树

人有枯梧树者,其邻人父言:

"枯梧之树不祥。"

其邻人遽而伐之。邻人父因请以为薪。

其人乃不悦曰:'邻人之父,徒欲为薪,而教吾伐之也,与我邻若此其险,岂可哉!'

—— 《列子》

FELLING THE PLANE TREE

A man had a withered plane tree.

"It's unlucky to keep a withered tree," said his neighbour.

But when the first man had felled the tree, his neighbour asked him for some of the wood as fuel.

"The old man simply wanted some fuel," thought the owner of the tree indignantly. "That's why he told me to fell me tree. We are neighbours, and yet he tricks me in this way—this is really going too far!"

Lie Zi

15

攫金不见人

昔齐人有欲金者。清旦,衣冠而之市,适鬻金者之所,因攫其金而去。

吏捕得之,问曰:"人皆在焉,子攫人之金何?"对曰:"取金之时,不见人,徒见金。"

—— 《列子》

THE MAN WHO SAW NOBODY

There was a man in the state of Qi who wanted some gold. One morning he dressed himself smartly and went to the market. Arriving at the gold-dealer's stall, he seized a piece of gold and made off.

The officer who caught him asked him: "Why did you steal gold in front of so many people?"

"When I took the gold, " he answered, "I saw nobody. All I saw was the gold."

Lie Zi

自满的马夫

晏子为齐相,出。其御之妻从门间而窥其夫为相御,拥大鞭盖,策驷马,意气杨杨,甚自得也。

既而归,其妻请去。夫问其故。

妻曰:"晏子,身相齐国。名显诸侯。今者妾观其出,志念深矣。常有以自下者。今子乃为人仆御。然子之意,自以为足。妾是以求去也。"

其后夫自抑损。

晏子怪而问之。御以实对。晏子荐以为大夫。

—— 《晏子春秋》

THE CONCEITED COACHMAN

One day Yan Zi, prime minister of the state of Qi, went out in his carriage. His coachman's wife, from her gate, saw her husband looking thoroughly smug and conceited under the great carriage awning as he drove his four horses.

When the coachman went home, his wife told him she wanted to leave him.

Her husband asked her why.

"Yan Zi is prime minister of Qi, " she replied. "He is famed throughout the states. But I saw him out today, deep in thought and not giving himself any airs. You are only a coachman, yet you look so conceited and pleased with yourself. That's why I want to leave you."

After this, her husband behaved more modestly. When Yan Zi, surprised, inquired the reason for this change, the coachman told him the truth. Then Yan Zi recommended him for an official post.

Yan Zi

叶公好龙

叶公子高好龙，居室文以像龙。

天龙闻而下之：窥颈于牖，拖尾于窗。

叶公见之，弃而还走，失其魂魄。

——是叶公非好龙也，好夫似龙而非

龙者也。

——《申子》

THE LORD WHO LOVED DRAGONS

Lord She was so fond of dragons that he had them painted and carved all over his house. When the real dragon in heaven heard about this, it flew down and put its head through Lord She's door and its tail through one of his windows. When the lord saw this he fled, frightened nearly out of his wits.

This shows that the lord was not really fond of dragons. He liked all that looked like dragons, but not the genuine thing.

Shen Zi

THE LORD WHO LOVED DRAGONS

黄金万两

　　齐人有东郭敬者，犹多愿，愿有万金。其徒请赒焉，不与，曰："吾将以求封也"。其徒怒而去之宋，曰："此爱于无也，故不如以先与之有也。"

——《商子》

THE THOUSAND TAELS OF GOLD

In the state of Qi there was one Mr. Dongguo Chang who was a man of many ambitions. Among other things, he wanted to possess ten thousand taels of gold.

A student of his, knowing of this ambition, asked to be favoured with a small sum, for he was very poor.

Mr. Dongguo Chang refused to grant his request. "I need all my money to buy myself a post in the government," he said.

His student became angry and left for the state of Song. Before he went he said to the teacher, "Since I shall have no share in the fortunes that you are coveting, I'd better seek them elsewhere. Maybe I can come by them earlier than you do."

Shang Zi

小鸟笑大鹏

　　有鸟焉,其名为鹏,背若泰山,翼若垂
天之云。搏扶羊角而上者九万里,绝云气,
负青天,然后图南,且适南冥也。

　　斥鷃笑之曰:"彼且奚适也? 我腾跃而
上,不过数仞而下,翱翔蓬蒿之间,此亦飞
之至也。而彼且奚适也?"

　　此小大之辩也。

——《庄子》

THE TOMTIT AND THE GIANT ROC

There was once a bird called the roc, whose back was as vast as Mount Tai and whose wings were like clouds that overspread the heavens. When it wheeled up into the air a whirlwind arose, and in each flight it covered ninety thousand *li*, soaring above the misty vapours under the azure sky. Once it was flying southwards to the Southern Ocean.

"Where can it be going?" wondered a tomtit with a laugh. "I leap up scores of feet, then come down to enjoy myself among the bushes. That's good enough for me. Where else does it want to go?"

Here we see the difference in outlook between great and small.

Zhuang Zi

不龟手之药

惠子谓庄子曰:"魏王贻我大瓠之种,我树之成而实五石,以盛水浆,其坚不能自举也。剖之以为瓢,则瓠落无所容。非不呺然大也。我为其无用而掊之。"

庄子曰:"夫子固拙于大用矣。宋人有善为不龟手之药者,世世以洴澼絖为事。客闻之,请买其方百金。聚族而谋曰:'我世世为洴澼絖,不过数金,今一朝而鬻技百金,请与之。'客得之以说吴王。越有难,吴王使之将,冬与越人水战,大败越人,裂地而封之。能不龟手一也,或以封,或不免于洴澼絖。则所用之异也。今子有五石之瓠,何不虑以为大樽,而浮于江湖,而忧其瓠落无所容? 则夫子犹有蓬之心也夫?"

—— 《庄子》

THE OINTMENT FOR CHAPPED HANDS

A family in the state of Song made an excellent ointment for chapped hands; so for generations they engaged in laundering. A man who heard of this offered a hundred pieces of gold for their recipe.

"We have been in the laundry trade for generations," said this family as they discussed the matter. "But we never made more than a few pieces of gold. Today we can sell our recipe for a hundred pieces. By all means let us sell it."

Now the state of Yue was invading the state of Wu, and having bought the recipe this man presented it to the Prince of Wu, who thereupon made him a general. His troops fought a naval action with those of Yue that winter, and completely routed the enemy. Then the prince made him a noble, rewarding him with a fief.

Thus the same ointment for chaps could win a fief or simply aid laundrymen.

All depends upon the use to which things are put.

Zhuang Zi

养 鸟

　　海鸟止于鲁郊。鲁候御而觞之于庙，
奏九韶以为乐，具太牢以为膳。鸟乃眩视
忧悲，不敢食一脔，不敢饮一杯，三日而死。

　　——此以己养养鸟也，非以鸟养养鸟
也。

——《庄子》

THE BIRD KILLED BY KINDNESS

A sea-gull alighted in a suburb of the capital of Lu. The Marquis of Lu welcomed it and feasted it in the temple hall, ordering the best music and grandest sacrifices for it. But the bird remained in a daze, looking quite wretched, not daring to swallow a morsel of meat or a single cup of wine. And after three days it died.

This was entertaining the sea-gull as the Marquis of Lu liked to be entertained, not as a sea-gull likes to be entertained.

Zhuang Zi

没有用途的本领

朱评漫学屠龙于支离益，单千金之家。三年技成，而无所用其巧。

——《庄子》

THE ART OF CARVING DRAGONS

Zhu Pingman went to Zhili Yi to learn how to carve dragons for the table. He studied for three years and spent all his very considerable property before he mastered the subject.

But he never found a dragon on which to practise his art.

Zhuang Zi

东施效颦

西施病心而颦其里。

其里之丑人，见而美之。妇亦捧心颦而其里。其里之富人见之，坚闭门而不出；贫人见之，挈妻子而去之走。

——彼知美颦，而不知颦之所美，惜乎！

—— 《庄子》

LEARNING THE WRONG THING

 Because Xi Shi, the famous beauty, suffered from heartburn, she would often frown in front of all the neighbours.

An ugly girl in the same village, who noticed this and thought it very charming, also put her hands to her breast and frowned in front of everyone. When the rich saw her, they barred their doors and would not come out. As for the poor, they ran away, taking their wives and children.

Poor thing! She could admire Xi Shi's frown, but did not know why it was beautiful.

Zhuang Zi

井 蛙

坎井之蛙谓东海之鳖曰:"吾乐与! 出跳梁乎井干之上,入休乎缺甃之崖;赴水则接腋持颐,蹶泥则没足灭跗;还虷蟹与科斗,莫吾能若也。且夫擅一壑之水,而跨跱坎井之乐,此亦至矣。夫子奚不时来入观乎?"

东海之鳖左足未入,而右膝已絷矣。于是逡巡而却,告之海曰:"夫千里之远,不足以举其大;千仞之高,不足以极其深。禹之时,十年九潦,而水弗为加益;汤之时,八年七旱,而崖不为加损。夫不为顷久推移,不以多少进退者,此亦东海之大乐也。"

THE FROG IN THE WELL

A frog lived in a shallow well.

"Look how well off I am here!" he told a big turtle from the Eastern Ocean. "I can hop along the coping of the well when I go out, and rest by a crevice in the bricks on my return. I can wallow to my heart's content with only my head above water, or stroll ankle deep through soft mud. No crabs or tadpoles can compare with me. I am master of the water and lord of this shallow well. What more can a fellow ask? Why don't you come here more often to have a good time?"

Before the turtle from the Eastern Ocean could get his left foot into the well, however, he caught his right claw on something. So he halted and stepped back, then began to describe the ocean to the frog.

"It's more than a thousand *li* across and more than ten thousand feet deep. In ancient times there were floods nine years out of ten yet the water in the ocean never increased. And later there were droughts seven years out of eight yet the water in the ocean never grew less. It has remained quite constant throughout the ag-

于是,坎井之蛙闻之,适适然惊,规规
然自失也。

——《庄子》

es. That is why I like to live in the Eastern Ocean."

Then the frog in the shallow well was silent and felt a little abashed.

Zhuang Zi

干车沟里的鲫鱼

庄周家贫,故往贷粟于监河候。

监河候曰:"诺!我将得邑金,将贷子三百金,可乎?"

庄周忿然作色曰:"周昨来,有中道而呼者。周顾视车辙中,有鲋鱼焉。周问之曰:'鲋鱼来!子何为者也?'对曰:'我,东海之波臣也。君岂有斗升之水而活我哉?'周曰:'诺!我且南游吴越之王,激西江之水,而迎子,可乎?'鲋鱼忿然作色曰:'吾失

THE CARP IN THE DRY RUT

When Zhuang Zi had no money, he went to the Lord Keeper of the River to borrow some grain.

"That's all right, " said the lord. "I shall soon have collected the taxes from my fief; then I'll lend you three hundred gold pieces. How about that?"

Very indignant, Zhuang Zi told him this story:

As I was coming here yesterday I heard a voice calling me, and looking round I saw a carp lying in a dry rut on the road.

"How did you get there, carp?"I asked.

"I am a native of the Eastern Ocean, " he replied. "Do you have a barrel of water to save my life?"

"That's all right, "I told him. "I shall soon be visiting the princes of Wu and Yue in the south, and I shall let through some water for you from the West River. How about that?"

The carp was most indignant.

我常与，我无所处。吾得斗升之水然活耳。
君乃言此，曾不如早索我于枯鱼之肆！'"

——《庄子》

"I am out of my usual element," he said, "and don't know what to do. One barrel of water would save me, but you give me nothing but empty promises. You'll have to look for me later in the fish market."

Zhuang Zi

都走失了羊群

臧与谷二人,相与牧羊,而俱亡其羊。

问臧奚事,则挟箧读书。

问谷奚事,则博塞以游。

二人者,事业不同,其于亡羊,均也。

—— 《庄子》

HOW TWO SHEPHERD BOYS
LOST THEIR SHEEP

Two shepherd boys, Gu and Zang, went out together with their flocks and both of them lost their sheep. When their master asked Zang what he had been doing, he answered that he had been reading. When Gu was questioned, he said he had been playing draughts.

They were doing different things, yet they both lost their sheep just the same.

Zhuang Zi

朝三暮四

宋有狙公者,爱狙,养之成群,能解狙之意;狙亦得公之心。

损其家口,充狙之欲。俄而匮焉,将限其食。恐众狙之不驯于己也,先诳之曰:"与若茅,朝三而暮四,足乎?"

众狙皆起而怒。

俄而曰:"朝四而暮三,足乎?"

众狙皆伏而喜。

—— 《庄子》

THREE CHESTNUTS OR FOUR

A monkey-trainer in the state of Song was fond of monkeys and kept a great many of them. He was able to understand them and they him. Indeed, he used to save some of his family's food for them. But a time came when there was not much food left at home, and he wanted to cut down the monkey's rations. He feared, however, they might not agree to this, and decided to deceive them.

"I'll give you three chestnuts each morning and four each evening, " he said. "Will that be enough?"

All the monkeys rose up to express their anger.

"Well, what about four in the morning and three in the evening?"he asked.

Then the monkeys squatted down again, feeling quite satisfied.

Lie Zi

国王拉弓

宣王好射，悦人之谓己能用强也。

其实所用不过三石。

以示左右，左右皆引试之，中关而止，皆曰：

"不下九石，非大王孰能用是。"

宣王悦之。

然则宣王用不过三石，而终身自以为九石。

三石，实也。九石，名也。

宣王悦其名而丧其实。

—— 《尹文子》

THE PRINCE AND HIS BOW

Prince Xuan was a keen archer and liked to be told what a powerful bowman he was, although he could draw no bow heavier than thirty catties. When he showed his bow to his attendants, they pretended to try to draw it, but merely bent it to half its full extent.

"This must weigh at least ninety catties!" they all cried. "None but Your Majesty could use such a bow."

And at this the prince was pleased.

Though he only used a thirty-catty bow, till the end of his life he believed that it weighed ninety catties. It was thirty in fact, and ninety merely in name; but for the sake of the empty name he sacrificed the truth.

Yin Wen Zi

47

学 棋

奕之为数,小数也。不专心致志,则不得也。

奕秋,通国之善奕者也。

使奕秋诲二人奕。

其一人,专心致志,惟奕秋之为听。

一人,虽听之,一心以为有鸿鹄将至,思援弓缴而射之。

虽与之俱学,弗若之矣。——为是其智弗若与?曰:"非然也。"

——《孟子》

LEARNING TO PLAY DRAUGHTS

Playing draughts is a minor art; yet even so, you must give your whole attention to it to learn it. Qiu, the best draughts-player in the country, had two pupils. One of them concentrated entirely on what Qiu told them, while the other, though he also listened to his master, was thinking all the time of the wild geese in the sky, and itching to get his bow and arrows to shoot them. So he did not learn as well as the other pupil. It was not because he was less intelligent.

Mencius

偷鸡的人

今有人,日攘邻人之鸡者。

或告之曰:"是非君子之道。"

曰:"请损之,月攘一鸡。以待来年,然后已。"

如知其非义,斯速已矣,何待来年?

—— 《孟子》

THE CHICKEN THIEF

There was a man who used to steal a chicken from his neighbours every day.

"It is wrong to steal, " someone told him.

"I'll cut down on it, " promised the chicken thief. "I shall steal one chicken a month from now on, and stop altogether next year."

Since he knew he was wrong, he ought to have stopped at once. Why wait for another year?

Mencius

拔苗助长

宋人有闵其苗之不长而揠之者。

芒芒然归,谓其人曰:"今日病矣! 予助苗长矣。"

其子趋而往视之,苗则槁矣。

——天下之不助苗长者寡矣:以为无益而舍之者,不耘苗者也;助之长者,揠苗者也。非徒无益,而又害之。

——《孟子》

HELPING YOUNG SHOOTS TO GROW

A man in the state of Song felt the shoots in his fields were not growing fast enough. So he pulled them all up, then went home quite exhausted.

"I'm tired out today," he told his family. "I've been helping the young shoots to grow."

His son ran out to the fields to have a look, and found all their seedlings were dead.

Most people would like to help young shoots to grow; but some think all efforts useless and make no attempt, not even weeding the fields; others try to help the shoots grow by pulling them up. This, of course, is worse than useless.

Mencius

胆小怕鬼的人

夏首之南,有人焉,曰涓蜀梁。其为人也,愚而善畏。明月而宵行,俯见其影,以为伏鬼也。仰视其发,以为立魅也。背而走,比至其家,失气而死。

——《荀子》

THE MAN WHO WAS AFRAID
OF GHOSTS

There was once a man of southern Xia Shou by the name of Juan Zhu Liang who was both slow-witted and cowardly.

Walking along a road one moonlit night, he saw his own shadow on the ground in front of him.

"It's a ghost crouching there!" he thought to himself.

Looking up, he saw a strand of hair dangling in front of his eyes.

"Ooh! It's standing up now!" he thought.

He was so frightened he turned around and began to shuffle backwards.

As soon as he reached his home, he dropped to the ground, dead.

Xun Zi

治 病

　　有医竘者，秦之良医也。为宣王割痤，为惠王疗痔，皆愈。

　　张子之背肿，命竘治之，谓竘曰："背非吾背也，任子制焉。"治之遂愈。

　　竘诚善治疾也，张子委制焉。

—— 《尸子》

DOCTOR AND PATIENT

Dr. Ju was a famous physician of the state of Qin. He had cut a tumour for Emperor Xuanwang and healed haemorrhoids for Emperor Huiwang.

A certain Mr. Zhang who was afflicted with a sore back asked the physician to treat it.

"I will not regard it as my back any longer. Do whatever you think fit with it!" he said.

Given a free hand, the physician cured his patient in no time.

There is no doubt that Dr. Ju was well versed in his craft, but the fact that Zhang put himself entirely in the doctor's hands also accounts for his prompt recovery.

Shi Zi

井里挖出一个活人

昔宋有丁氏，家故无井，而出溉汲焉。常一日而一人基外，惩其如是也，鸠工而穿井于庭。

家相语曰："今吾之穿井于庭，得一人矣。"

有闻而传之曰：丁氏穿井而得一人也。国人更相道之，语彻于宋君。召其人质之。

丁氏对曰："自臣穿井，家得一人之力矣，非得一人于井也。"

—— 《子华子》

THE MAN WHO WAS FOUND
IN THE WELL

The Ding family in the state of Song had no well of its own. Someone in the family sometimes had to spend a whole day doing nothing but fetch water from a distance.

To save trouble, they had a well sunk in their courtyard.

After the job was finished, they said to one an other happily, "It seems with the sinking of the well one more person is added to our household."

One of Ding's friends heard of the remark and the word passed from that friend to that friend's friend and yet to another, until the story ran as follows: "The Dings had a well sunk and found a man inside!"

When the Duke of Song heard the tale he sent for Ding to inquire into the matter.

"With the sinking of the well it is as though your obedient servant has secured the help of a man, " explained Ding to the duke, "it isn't that I actually found a man in the well."

Zi Hua Zi

刻舟求剑

楚人有涉江者,其剑自舟中坠于水。

逐契其舟,曰:"是我剑之所以坠。"

舟止,从其所契者入水求之。

——舟已行矣,而剑不行:求剑若此,
不亦惑乎?

——《吕氏春秋》

MARKING THE BOAT TO
LOCATE THE SWORD

A man of the state of Chu was ferrying across a river when his sword fell into the water. He lost no time in marking the side of the boat.

"This is where my sword dropped, " he said.

When the boat morred, he got into the water to look for his sword by the place which he had marked. But since the boat had moved while the sword had not, this method of locating his sword proved unsuccessful.

The Discourses of Lü Buwei
(*Lü Shi Chun Qiu*)

游泳名手的儿子

　　有过于江上者,见人方引婴儿,而欲投之江中,婴儿啼。

　　人问其故。

　　曰:"此其父善游。"

　　——其父虽善游,其子岂遽善游哉!

——《吕氏春秋》

THE SON OF A GOOD SWIMMER

A man walking along the river bank saw someone about to throw a small boy into the water. The child was screaming with terror.

"Why do you want to throw that child into the river?" asked the passer-by.

"His father is a good swimmer," was the answer.

But it does not follow that the son of a good swimmer can swim.

The Discourses of Lü Buwei

掩耳盗钟

范氏之亡也,百姓有得钟者。

欲负而走,则钟大不可负。

以椎毁之,钟况然有音。恐人闻之而夺己也,逐掩其耳。

——恶人闻之,可也;恶己自闻之,悖矣。

—— 《吕氏自知》

STEALING THE BELL

After the fall of the house of Fan, a man got hold of a bronze bell. It was too big to carry away on his back, and when he tried to break it with a hammer it made such a din that he feared others might hear and take it away from him. So he hastily stopped his ears.

It was all right to worry about others hearing the noise, but foolish to stop his own ears.

The Discourses of Lü Buwei

赶 马

　　宋人有取道者,其马不进,倒而投之溪水,又复取道,其马不进,又倒而投之溪水,如此者三。

　　虽造父之所以威马,不过此矣,不得造父之道,而徒得其威;无益于御。

—— 《吕氏春秋》

PUNISHING THE HORSE

Because his horse refused to advance, a traveller in the state of Song drove it into a stream, then mounted to set off again. Still the horse refused to go, and he punished it once more in the same way. This happened three times in all. Even the most skilful rider could devise no better means of frightening a horse; but if you are not a rider, simply a bully, your horse will refuse to carry you.

The Discourses of Lü Buwei

聪明的老妈妈

臣里母相善妇,见疑盗肉,其姑去之。恨而告于里母。

里母曰:"安行? 今令姑呼汝!"

即束蕴请火去妇之家曰:"吾犬争肉相杀,请火治之。"

姑乃直使人逐去妇还之。

——故里母非谈说之士;束蕴请火,非还妇之道也;然物有所感,事有可适。

—— 《韩诗外传》

THE CLEVER OLD WOMAN

An old woman was friendly with a young wife, whose mother-in-law suspected her of stealing some meat and wanted to drive her away. In despair she went to complain to the old woman.

"Where can you go?" demanded her old neighbour. "I shall get your mother-in-law to call you back."

Then she took a bundle of straw to the house where the young woman lived.

"My dogs are fighting over some stolen meat, " she said. "So I want to light a fire to give them a beating."

As soon as the mother-in-law heard that, she sent to recall her daughter-in-law.

This old woman was not gifted with eloquence, and taking a bundle of straw to ask for a light is not the usual means of effecting a reconciliation; but when you do the right thing you achieve results.

Han Ying's Commentary on the Book of Songs

画什么东西最难

客有为齐王画者,齐王问曰:"画孰最难者?"曰:"犬马最难。""孰最易者?"曰:"鬼魅最易。"夫犬马,人所知也,旦暮罄于前,不可类之,故难;鬼神,无形者,不罄于前,故易之也。

—— 《韩非子》

PAINTING GHOSTS

There was an artist who worked for the prince of Qi.

"Tell me, "said the prince, " what are the hardest things to paint?"

"Dogs, horses, and the like, " replied the artist.

"What are the easiest?" asked the prince.

"Ghosts and monsters, " the artist told him. "We all know dogs and horses and see them every day; but it is hard to make an exact likeness of them. That is why they are difficult subjects. But ghosts and monsters have no definite form, and no one has ever seen them; so they are easy to paint."

Han Fei Zi

坏　墙

宋有富人,大雨坏墙。

其子曰:"不筑,必将有盗。"

其邻人之父亦云。

暮而果大亡其财。

其家甚智其子,而疑邻人之父。

——《韩非子》

THE CRUMBLING WALL

There was once a rich man in the state of Song. After a downpour of rain his wall began to crumble.

"If you don't mend that wall, " warned his son, "a thief will get in."

An old neighbour gave the same advice.

That night, indeed, a great deal of money was stolen. Then the rich man commended his son's intelligence, but suspected his old neighbour of being the thief.

Han Fei Zi

象　箸

　　昔者纣为象箸，而箕子怖。以为象箸
必不加于土铏，必须犀玉之杯。象箸玉杯
必不羹菽藿，则必旄象豹胎。旄象豹胎，必
不衣短褐而食于茅屋之下，则锦衣九重，广
室高台。吾畏其卒，故怖其始。居五年，纣
为肉圃，设炮烙，登糟邱，临酒池，纣遂以
亡。故箕子见象箸以知天下之祸。故曰，
见小曰明。

——《韩非子》

IVORY CHOPSTICKS

When King Zhou ordered chopsticks made of ivory, Ji Zi was most perturbed. For he feared that once the king had ivory chopsticks he would not be content with earthenware, but would want cups of rhinoceros horn and jade; and instead of beans and vegetables, he would hardly be willing either to wear rough homespun or live under a thatched roof, but would demand silks and splendid mansions.

"It is fear of what this will lead to, " said Ji Zi, "that upsets me."

Five years later, indeed, King Zhou had a garden filled with meat, tortured his subjects with hot irons, and caroused in a lake of wine. And so he lost his kingdom.

Han Fei Zi

曾参杀猪

　　曾子之妻之市,其子随之而泣。其母曰:"女还,愿反为女杀彘。"

　　妻适市来,曾子欲捕彘杀之。

　　妻止之曰:"特与婴儿戏耳。"

　　曾子曰:"婴儿非与戏也!婴儿非有知也,待父母而学者也,听父母之教。今子欺之,是教子欺也。母欺子,子而不信其母,非以成教也。"

　　遂烹彘也。

—— 《韩非子》

WHY ZENG SHEN KILLED THE PIG

One day, when Zeng Shen's wife was going to the market, their son cried and clamoured to go with her.

"Go back now!" she wheedled him. "When I get home we'll kill the pig for you."

Upon her return, she found Zeng Shen about to kill the pig. She hastily stopped him.

"I didn't really mean it," she protested. "I just said that to keep the boy quiet."

"How can you deceive a child like that?" asked Zeng Shen. "Children know nothing to begin with, but they copy their parents and learn from them. When you cheat the boy, you are teaching him to lie. If a mother deceives her child, he will not trust her, and that is no way to bring him up."

So he killed the pig after all.

Han Fei Zi

滥竽充数

　　齐宣王使人吹竽,必三百人。

　　南郭处士请为王吹竽。宣王说之,廪食以数百人。

　　宣王死,湣王立,好一一听之。

　　处士逃。

—— 《韩非子》

THE MAN WHO PRETENDED HE
COULD PLAY REED PIPES

When Prince Xuan of Qi called for reed pipe music, he would have three hundred men playing at the same time. Then a scholar named Nanguo asked for a place in the orchestra, and the prince, taking a fancy to him, gave him a salary large enough to feed several hundred men.

After Prince Xuan's death, however, Prince Min came to the throne, and he liked solo performances.

There upon the scholar fled.

Han Fei Zi

自相矛盾

　　楚有鬻盾与矛者。誉之曰:"吾盾之坚,物莫能陷也。"又誉其矛曰:"吾矛之利,于物无不陷也。"

　　或曰:"以子之矛,陷子之盾,何如?"

　　其人弗能应也。

—— 《韩非子》

THE MAN WHO SOLD
SPEARS AND SHIELDS

In the state of Chu lived a man who sold shields and spears.

"My shields are so strong, "he boasted, "that nothing can pierce them. My spears are so sharp there is nothing they cannot pierce."

"What if one of your spears strikes one of your shields?" someone asked him.

The man had no answer to that.

Han Fei Zi

买　鞋

　　郑人有且置履者,先自度其足而置之
其坐。

　　至之市,而忘操之,已得履,乃曰:"吾
忘持度。"反归取之。

　　乃反,市罢,遂不得履。

　　人曰:"何不试之以足?"

　　曰:"宁信度,无自信也"。

——《韩非子》

BUYING A PAIR OF SHOES

A man in the state of Zheng decided to buy some new shoes. He measured his feet but left the measure on his seat, and went to the market without it. There he found a shoemaker.

"Why, I forgot to bring the measurement!" he cried.

He hurried home to fetch it.

By the time he got back to the market, the fair was over; so he failed to buy his shoes.

"Why didn't you try the shoes on?" asked one of his neighbours.

"I trust the ruler more," was his reply.

Han Fei Zi

长生不老的仙方

客有教燕王为不死之道者，王使人学之，所使学者未及学，而客死，王大怒诛之。王不知客之欺己，而诛学者之晚也，夫信不然之物，而诛无罪之臣，不察之患也，且人所急无如其身，不能自使其无死，安能使王长生哉！

——《韩非子》

A RECIPE FOR IMMORTALITY

A stranger informed the Prince of Yan that he could make him immortal, and the prince bade one of his subjects learn this art; but before the man could do so the stranger died. Then the prince, in great anger, executed his subject.

He failed to see that the stranger was cheating him, but taken in by his lies had an innocent citizen killed. This shows what a fool he was! For a man values nothing more than his own life, yet this fellow could not even keep himself alive, so what could he do for the prince?

Han Fei Zi

酒和恶狗

宋人有酤酒者,升概甚平,遇客甚谨,多酒甚美,县帜甚高:然而不售——酒酸。

怪其故。问其所知闾长者杨倩。

倩曰:"汝狗猛耶?"

曰:"狗猛,则酒何故而不售?"

曰:"人畏焉!或令孺子怀钱挈壶而往酤,而狗迓而龁之,此酒所以酸而不售也。"

——《韩非子》

THE DOG WHO SOURED WINE

There was a brewer in the state of Song whose wine was excellent. He gave fair measure, was civil to his customers, and has his sign up in a most conspicuous place. Yet he could not sell his wine, which was said to be sour. He asked an elder whom he knew well, what the reason for this was.

"Is your dog fierce?" asked the elderly man.

"As a matter of fact, it is, " replied the brewer. "But what has that to do with my wine not selling?"

"People are afraid of your dog. When a boy is sent with money and a pot to buy your wine, the dog rushes out to bite him. That is why your wine turns sour and will not sell."

Han Fei Zi

守株待兔

宋人有耕田者。田中有株。兔走触株,折颈而死。因释其耒耒而守株,冀复得兔。

——兔不可复得,而身为宋国笑。

—— 《韩非子》

WAITING FOR A HARE TO TURN UP

There was a peasant in the state of Song. One day a hare dashed up, knocked against a tree in his field, broke its neck and fell dead. Then the peasant put down his hoe and waited by the tree for another hare to turn up. No more hares appeared, however; but he became the laughing-stock of the state.

Han Fei Zi

水蛇搬家

涸泽蛇将徙,有小蛇谓大蛇曰:

"子行而我随之,人以为蛇之行者耳,必有杀子,不如相衔负我以行,人以我为神君也。"乃相衔负以越公道。

人皆避之曰:

"神君也"。

—— 《韩非子》

HOW TWO WATER SNAKES
MOVED HOUSE

The snakes wanted to move away from a marsh which was drying up.

"If you lead the way and I follow, " said a small to a large snake, "men will know we are moving away and someone will kill you. You had better carry me on your back, each holding the other's tail in his mouth. Then men will think I am a god."

So, each holding the other, they crossed the highway. And everybody made way for them, crying out: "This is a god!"

Han Fei Zi

弓与箭

一人曰:"吾弓良,无所用矢。"

一人曰:"吾矢善,无所用弓。"

羿闻之曰:"非弓何以往矢? 非矢何以中的?"

会合弓矢,而教之射。

—— 《韩非子》

THE BOW AND THE ARROW

One man boasted, "My bow is so good, it needs no arrow."

Another man boasted, "My arrow is so good, it needs no bow."

The skilled archer Yi heard them and said, "Without a bow, how can you shoot an arrow? And without an arrow how can you hit the target?"

So the bow and the arrow were used together, and Yi taught these men to shoot.

Han Fei Zi

买椟还珠

楚人有卖其珠于郑者,为木兰之柜,熏以桂椒,缀以珠玉,饰以玫瑰,辑以翡翠。

郑人买其椟而还其珠。

此可谓善卖椟矣,未可谓善鬻珠也。

—— 《韩非子》

SELLING THE CASKET
WITHOUT THE PEARLS

A native of the state of Chu decided to sell some pearls in the state of Zheng. He had a casket made of rare wood, scented it with spices, inlaid it with jade and other precious jewels, and wrapped it in kingfishers ' plumage. The result was that the men of Zheng were eager to buy the casket, but he could not sell his pearls.

This fellow may be considered a skilled casket seller, but deserves no credit at all as a seller of pearls.

Han Fei Zi

羊蒙虎皮

羊质而虎皮,见草而说,见豺而战。忘其皮之虎矣。

——《法言》

THE LAMB IN A TIGER'S SKIN

Once a lamb clad itself in a tiger's skin.

As it was stalking along, it bleated joyously at the sight of the green grass, but when it saw a wolf in the distance it trembled all over.

The truth is that the lamb had forgotten that it had the tiger's skin on.

Fan Yan

鹬蚌相争

蚌方出曝,而鹬啄其肉。蚌合而拑其喙。

鹬曰:"今日不雨,明日不雨,既有死蚌!"

蚌亦谓鹬曰:"今日不出,明日不出,既有死鹬!"

两者不肯相舍,渔者得而并禽之。

——《战国策》

THE SNIPE AND THE MUSSEL

A mussel was opening its shell to bask in the sun when a snipe pecked at it. The mussel clamped down on the bird's beak, and held it fast.

"If it doesn't rain today or tomorrow," said the snipe, "there will be a dead mussel lying here."

"If you can't pry loose today or tomorrow," retorted the mussel, "there will be a dead snipe here too."

As neither of them would give way, a passing fisherman caught them both.

Warring States Anecdotes

狐假虎威

虎求百兽而食之,得狐。

狐曰:"子无敢食我也!天帝使我长百兽;今子食我,是逆天帝命也。子以我为不信,吾为子先行,子随我后,观百兽之见我而敢不走乎!"

虎以为然,故遂与之行。兽见之皆走。

虎不知兽畏已而走也,以为畏狐也。

—— 《战国策》

THE FOX WHO PROFITED
BY THE TIGER'S MIGHT

While hunting for prey, the tiger caught a fox.

"You can't eat me, "said the fox. "The Emperor of Heaven has appointed me king of the beasts. If you eat me, you'll be disobeying his orders. If you don't believe me, follow me. You'll soon see whether the other animals run away at the sight of me or not."

Agreeing to this, the tiger accompanied; and when all the beasts saw them coming they dashed away. Not realizing that they were afraid of him, the tiger thought they were afraid of the fox.

Warring States Anecdotes

曾参杀人

　　昔曾子处费,费人有与曾子同名族者,而杀人。

　　人告曾子母曰:"曾参杀人!"

　　曾子之母曰:"吾子不杀人!"织自若。

　　有顷焉,人又曰:"曾参杀人!"

　　其母尚织自若也。

　　顷之,一人又告之曰:"曾参杀人!"

　　其母惧,投杼,谕逾墙而走。

——《战国策》

THE RUMOUR ABOUT ZENG SHEN

Once, when Zeng Shen went to the district of Fei, a man with the same name there committed a murder. Someone went to tell Zeng Shen's mother: "Zeng Shen has killed a man!"

"Impossible, " she replied. "My son would never do such a thing."

She went calmly on with her weaving.

After a while, someone else came to report: "Zeng Shen has killed a man."

Still the old lady went on weaving.

Then a third man came to tell her: "Zeng Shen has killed a man!"

This time his mother was frightened. She threw down her shuttle and escaped over the wall.

For although Zeng Shen was a good man and his mother trusted him, when three men accused him of murder, much as she loved him she couldnot but begin to doubt him.

Warring States Anecdotes

南辕北辙

魏王欲攻邯郸。季梁闻之,中道而反,衣焦不申,头尘不去,往见王曰:

"今者臣来,见人于大行,方北面而持其驾。告臣曰:'我欲之楚。'臣曰:'君之楚,将奚为北面?'曰:'吾马良。'臣曰:'马虽良,此非楚之路也。'曰:'吾用多。'臣曰:'用虽多,此非楚之路也。'曰:'吾御者善。'此数者愈善,而离楚愈远耳!……"

——《战国策》

THE WRONG DIRECTION

The Prince of Wei decided to invade Handan, the capital of the state of Zhao. Although Qiliang was on a journey when he heard this, he turned back at once and, without waiting to smooth his crumpled garments or brush the dust from his head, went to see the king.

"On my way back, " he said, "I came across a man at Taihang Mountain, who was riding northwards. He told me he was going to the state of Chu."

"'In that case, why are you heading north? 'I asked him.

"'That's all right, 'he replied. 'I have good horses. '

"'Your horses may be good, but your're taking the wrong direction. '

"'Well, I have plenty of money. '

"'You may have plenty of money, but this is the wrong direction. '

"'Well, I have an excellent charioteer. '

"'The better your horses, 'I told him, 'the more money you have and the more skilled your charioteer, the further you will get from the state of Chu. '"

Warring States Anecdotes

画蛇添足

　　楚有祠者,赐其舍人卮酒。舍人相谓曰:"数人饮之不足,一人饮之有余。请画地为蛇,先成者饮酒。"

　　一人蛇先成,引酒且饮之。乃左手持卮,右手画蛇曰:"吾能为之足。"

　　未成。一人之蛇成,夺其卮曰:"蛇固无足,子安得为之足!"遂饮其酒。

　　为蛇足者终亡其酒。

—— 《战国策》

DRAWING A SNAKE WITH LEGS

In the state of Chu, a man who had held a sacrifice gave the goblet of sacrificial wine to his stewards.

"This is not enough for us all, " said the stewards, "but more than enough for one. Let's draw snakes on the ground, and the one who finishes first can have the wine."

The man who finished first picked up the goblet, but holding it in his left hand went on drawing with his right.

"I am adding some legs, " he said.

Before he finished the legs, though, another steward completed his drawing and took the goblet from him.

"A snake has no legs, " said this last. "Why should you add legs?"

So he drained the wine instead. And the one who had drawn the legs had nothing to drink.

Warring States Anecdotes

借 光

江上之处女,有家贫而烛者。

处女相与语,欲去之。

家贫无烛者将去矣,谓处女曰:"妾以无烛故,常先至扫室布席。何爱余明之照四壁者,幸以赐妾,何妨于处女?妾自以有益于处女,何为去我?"

处女相语,以为然而留之。

—— 《战国策》

BORROWING THE LIGHT

A girl in one of the workshops by the river was too poor to buy oil for the lamp; so the other girls decided to drive her away. As the poor girl was leaving she said to the others:

"Because I couldn't afford to pay for the light, I always arrived first to sweep the room and put down the mats. Your light shines on all four walls: Why grudge me a share in it? It doesn't hurt you to let me borrow your light, and I make myself useful to you. Why should you drive me away?"

Realizing the truth of what she said, they let her stay after all.

Warring States Anecdotes

邹忌比美

　　邹忌修八尺有余,而形貌昳丽,朝服衣冠,窥镜,谓其妻曰:"我与城北徐公孰美?"其妻曰:"君美甚,徐公何能及君也!"——城北徐公,齐国之美丽者也。忌不自信,而复问其妾曰:"吾与徐公孰美?"妾曰:"徐公何能及君也!"旦日,客从外来,与坐谈,问之:"吾与徐公孰美?"客曰:"徐公不若君之美也。"明日,徐公来。孰视之,自以为不如;窥镜而自视,又弗为远甚。暮寝而思之

WHICH WAS THE MORE HANDSOME

Lord Zou Ji of the state of Qi was six feet tall and a fine figure of a man. One morning he dressed himself smartly, and studied himself in the mirror.

"Which is more handsome, " he asked his wife, "Lord Xu of the north city or I?"

"You are ever so handsome, " replied his wife. "How can Lord Xu compare with you?"

Since Lord Xu of the north city was famed for his good looks throughout the state, Zou Ji did not altogether believe his wife. He repeated his question to his concubine.

"How can Lord Xu compare with you?" cried the concubine.

Later that morning a protégé came in, and Zou Ji put the same question to him.

"You are by far the more handsome, " replied this man.

The next day Lord Xu called, and a careful scrutiny convinced Zou Ji that Xu's good looks far surpassed his. He studied himself in the mirror, and undoubtedly he was the plainer of the two.

曰:"吾妻之美我者,私我也;妾之美我者,畏我也;客之美我者,欲有求于我也。"

——《战国策》

That night in bed he reached the following conclusion: "My wife said I was more handsome because she is biased. My concubine said so because she is afraid. And my protégé said so because he wants something from me!"

Warring States Anecdotes

千里马

古之君人，有以千金求千里马者，三年不能得。

涓人言于君曰："请求之。"

君遣之，三月得千里马，马已死，买其首五百金，反以报君。

君大怒曰："所求者生马，安事死马，而捐五百金。"

涓人对曰："死马且买之五百金，况生马乎？天下必以王为能市马，马今至矣。"

于是不能期年，千里之马至者三。

—— 《战国策》

BUYING A GOOD HORSE

There was a king who was willing to pay a thousand pieces of gold for a horse that could run a thousand *li* without stopping. For three years he tried in vain to find such a steed.

Then someone offered: "let me look for a horse for your Majesty."

Then king agreed to this.

After three months this man came back, having spent five hundred pieces of gold on a horse's skull.

The king was most enraged.

"I want a live horse!" he roared. "What use is a dead horse to me? Why spend five hundred pieces of gold on nothing?"

But the man replied: "If you will spend five hundred pieces of gold on a dead horse, won't you give much more for a live one? When people hear of this, they will know you are really willing to pay for a good horse, and will quickly send you their best."

Sure enough, in less than a year the king succeeded in buying three excellent horses.

Warring States Anecdotes

泥人和木偶

　　孟尝君将入秦,止者千数而弗听,苏秦欲止之。孟尝君曰:"人事者吾已尽知之矣,吾所未闻者独鬼事耳。"苏秦曰:"臣之来也,固不取言人事也,固且以鬼事相见君。"孟尝君见之。谓孟尝君曰:"今者臣来,过于淄上,有土偶人与桃梗相与语。桃梗谓土偶人曰:'子,西岸之土也,挺子以为人,至此八月,降雨下,淄水至,则汝残矣。'土偶曰:'不然,吾西岸之土也,吾残,则覆西岸耳。今子,东国之桃梗也,刻削子之为人,降雨下,淄水至,流子而去,则子漂漂者

THE CLAY FIGURE AND
THE WOODEN IMAGE

When Lord Mengchang decided to leave his native land—the state of Qi—to take office in the state of Qin, hundreds of men tried to dissuade him from going. But he would not listen to them. Then Su Jin, the rhetorician, wanted to reason with him.

"I have heard all the arguments men can think of, " said Lord Mengchang. "All that's lacking is some supernatural reasoning."

"I came here with no intention of discussing human affairs, " replied Su Jin. "I am asking for an audience to speak of the supernatural."

Then the lord admitted him, and Su Jin told the following story:

"Passing the River Zi on my way here, I heard a clay figure and a peach-wood image talking together.

" 'You used to be a piece of clay on the west bank, ' jeered the wooden image. 'Now you have been made into a figure. But druing the big rains in the eighth month, when the river rises, you are sure to be destroyed. '

" 'What of it? ' retorted the clay figure. 'I come from the west bank, and when I am destroyed I shall become part of it again. But you are made of peach wood from the east country, carved into an image. When the great rains come and the river rises, you will be swept away, and then what will you do? '

将何如耳?'今秦四塞之国,譬若虎口,而君入之,则臣不知君所出矣。"孟尝君乃止。

——《战国策》

"The state of Qin has strong passes on every side, so to enter it is like entering a tiger's mouth! Once you go to Qin, I fear you will never come back."

Then the lord gave up his plan.

Warring States Anecdotes

猫头鹰搬家

　　枭逢鸠。鸠曰:"子将安之?"枭曰:"我将东徙。"鸠曰:"何故?"枭曰:"乡人皆恶我鸣,以故东徙。"鸠曰:"子能更鸣可矣;不能更鸣,东徙,犹恶子之声。"

—— 《说苑》

THE OWL MOVES HOUSE

One day the owl met the turtle-dove.

"Where are you going?" inquired the dove.

"I am moving east, " said the owl.

"Why is that?" asked the dove.

"All the people here dislike my hoot, " replied the owl. "That is why I want to move east."

"If you can change your voice, " said the dove, "then it will be all right. But if you can't, even if you move east, the people there will dislike you just the same."

The Garden of Anecdotes (*Shuo Yuan*)

比 喻

　　客谓梁王曰:"惠子之言事也,善譬,王使无譬,则不能言矣。"王曰:"诺。"明日见,谓惠子曰:"愿先生言事则直言耳,无譬也!"惠子曰:"今有人于此而不知弹者,曰:'弹之状若何?'应曰:'弹之状为弹。'则喻乎?"王曰:"未谕也。""子是更应曰:'弹之状为弓,而以竹为弦。'则知乎?"王曰:"可知矣。"惠子曰:"夫说者固以其所知谕其所

THE USE OF PARABLES

"Hui Zi is forever using parables," complained someone to the Prince of Liang. "If you, sire, forbid him to speak in parables, he won't be able to make his meaning clear."

The prince agreed with this man.

The next day the prince saw Hui Zi.

"From now on," he said, "kindly talk in a straightforward manner, and not in parables."

"Suppose there were a man who did not know what a catapult is," replied Hui Zi. "If he asked you what it looked like, and you told him it looked just like a catapult, would he understand what you meant?"

"Of course not," answered the prince.

"But suppose you told him that a catapult looks something like a bow and that it is made of bamboo – wouldn 't he understand you better?"

"Yes, that would be clearer," admitted the prince.

"We compare something a man does not know with something he does know in order to help him to under-

不知而使人知之，公子曰‘无譬’，则不可矣。"王曰："美善。"

——《说苑》

stand it, " said Hui Zi. "If you won't let me use parables, how can I make things clear to you?"

The prince agreed that he was right.

The Garden of Anecdotes

好学的三个比喻

晋平公问于师旷曰:

"吾年七十,欲学,恐已暮矣。"

师旷曰:"何不炳烛乎?"

平公曰:"安有为人臣而戏其君乎?"

师旷曰:"盲臣安敢戏(其)君(乎),臣闻之:少而好学,如日出之阳;壮而好学,如日中之光;老而好学,如炳烛之明:炳烛之明,孰与昧行乎?"

平公曰:"善哉!"

—— 《说苑》

A PARABLE ON STUDY

"I am seventy already, " said Duke Ping of Jin to his blind musician Shi Kuang. "Though I want very much to study and read some books, I feel it is too late."

"But why not light the candle?" suggested Shi Kuang.

"How dare a subject joke with his master?" cried the duke angrily.

"A blind musician, I dare not!" protested Shi Kuang. "But I have heard that if a man is fond of study in his youth, his future is as bright as the morning sun; if he applies himself to study in middle age, it is like the noon-day sun; while if he begins to study when he is old, it is like a candle's flame. Though a candle is not very bright, at least it is better than groping in the dark."

The duke agreed with him.

The Garden of Anecdotes

龙王变鱼

昔白龙下清冷之渊化为鱼，渔者豫且射中其目，白龙上诉天帝，天帝曰：

"当是之时若安置而形?"白龙对曰："我下清冷之渊化为鱼。"天帝曰："鱼固人之所射也，若是豫且何罪?"

—— 《说苑》

THE DRAGON WHO CHANGED
INTO A FISH

Once the white dragon went down from heaven to a cool lake, taking the form of a fish. Then a fisherman shot at him and pierced him in the eye. The white dragon flew up at once to complain to the Emperor of Heaven.

"I took the form of a fish when I went down to the lake."

"Then of course a fisherman would try to catch you. How can you blame him?"

The Garden of Anecdotes

蝉、螳螂、黄雀

园中有树，其上有蝉。

蝉方奋翼悲鸣，欲饮清露，不知螳螂之在其后，曲其颈，欲攫而食之。

螳螂方欲食蝉，而不知黄雀在后，举其颈，欲啄而食之也。

黄雀方欲食螳螂，不知童子挟弹丸在下，迎而欲弹之。

—— 《说苑》

THE CICADA, THE PRAYING MANTIS AND THE SPARROW

There is a tree in the garden, and on it there is a cicada. This cicada perches up there, chirping away and drinking the dew, not knowing that there is a praying mantis behind it. And the praying mantis leans forward, raising its forelegs to catch the cicada, not knowing that there is a sparrow beside it. The sparrow, again, cranes its neck to peck at the praying mantis, not knowing that there is someone with a catapult waiting below.

The Garden of Anecdotes

铁 甲

田赞衣儒衣而见荆王,荆王曰:"先生之衣,何其恶也?"赞对曰:"衣又有恶此者。"荆王曰:"可得而闻耶?"对曰:"甲恶于此"。王曰:"何谓也?"对曰"冬日则寒,夏日则热,衣无恶于甲者矣;赞贫,故衣恶也。今大王万乘之主也,富厚无敌,而好衣人以甲,臣窃为大王不取也。意者为其义耶?甲兵之事折人之首,刳人之腹,堕人城郭,系人子女,其名尤甚不荣;意者为其贵耶?苟虑害人,人亦必虑害之,苟虑危人,人亦必虑危之,其贵人甚不安;之二者,为大王

ON WEARING ARMOUR

One day Tian Zan went into the presence of the Prince of Chu in rags.

"You are very shabbily dressed, sir, " remarked the prince.

"There are worse clothes than these, " replied Tian Zan.

"What may they be, pray?"

"Armour is worse. "

"What do you mean by that?"

"It is cold in winter and hot in summer; so no clothes are worse than armour. Since I am a poor man, my clothes are naturally shabby; but you are a prince with ten thousand chariots and untold wealth, yet you like to dress men in armour. This is something I cannot understand. Perhaps you are bent on fame? But armour is used in war, when men's heads are hacked off, their bodies pierced, their cities razed to the ground, and their parents and children tortured—the mere name is rather inglorious. Or perhaps you are bent on gain? But if you try to injure others, others will try to injure you; and if you endanger their lives, they will endanger yours. Thus you will gain nothing but trouble for your

无取焉。"荆王无以应也。

——《新序》

own men. If I were you, I would not wage war for either."

The Prince of Chu had nothing to say to that.

New Discourses (*Xin Xu*)

皮之不存，毛将焉附

魏文侯出游，见路人反裘而负刍。

文侯曰："胡为反裘而负刍?"

对曰："臣爱其毛"。

文侯曰："若不知其里尽而毛无所恃
也?"

—— 《新序》

THE FUR AND THE HIDE

While on a tour of the country, Marquis Wen of the state of Wei saw a man wearing a fur with the hide outside, carrying a bundle of straw.

"Why wear your fur inside out to carry straw?" asked the marquis.

"To protect the fur, " was the answer.

"Don't you realize, man, " said the marquis, "that when the hide wears out, the fur will go too?"

New Discourses

谁该坐上座

　　客有过主人者,见其灶直突,傍有积薪。客谓主人:"更为曲突,远徙其薪。不者,且有火患。"主人嘿然不应。俄而家果失火。邻里共救之,幸而得息。于是杀牛置酒,谢其邻人:灼烂者在于上行,余客以功次座。而不录言曲突者。人谓主人曰:"乡使听客之言,不费牛酒,终无火患。今论功而请宾,曲突徙薪之恩泽,焦头烂额为

WHO DESERVED THE PLACE
OF HONOUR?

A man passing a friend's house noticed that the kitchen chimney was straight, and a pile of fuel was stacked beside the stove.

"You had better build another chimney with a bend in it," he advised the householder. "and move that fuel away, otherwise it may catch fire."

But the master of the house ignored his advice.

Later the house did catch fire; but luckily the neighbours came and helped to put it out. Then that family killed an ox and prepared wine to express their thanks to the neighbours. Those who had received burns were seated in the places of honour, and the rest according to their merit; but no mention was made of the man who had advised them to build a new chimney.

"If you had taken that man's advice," someone said to the master of the house, "you could have saved the expense of the ox and wine, and avoided a fire. Now you are entertaining your friends to thank them for what they did. But is it right to ignore the man who advised you to rebuild the chimney and move the firewood, while you treat those who received burns as guests of honour?"

上客耶?"主人乃寤而请之。

——《汉书》

Then the master of the house realized his mistake, and invited the man who had given him good advice.

The Han Dynasty History

对牛弹琴

　　公明仪为牛弹清角之操,伏食为故,非牛不闻,不合其耳矣。转为蚊虻之声,孤犊之鸣,即掉尾,奋耳、蹀躞而听。

——《牟子》

PLAYING THE HARP TO AN OX

One day Gong Mingyi, the celebrated musician, was playing an elegant tune on his harp to amuse a browsing ox.

The ox, however, continued to munch, paying no heed to him at all.

Then he struck up some different notes, which sounded like mosquitoes droning and calves bleating. Whereupon the ox flicked its tail, pricked up its ears, and began frisking round and round, evidently absorbed in the music.

Mou Zi

哭妈妈

东家母死，其子哭之不哀。西家子见之，归谓其母曰："社何爱速死？吾必悲哭社。"

其欲其母之死者，虽死也不能悲哭矣。

——《淮南子》

LAMENTING A MOTHER'S DEATH

The mother of a man living in the east of a village died, and he lamented her death: but he did not sound too sad. When the son of a woman living in the west of the village saw this, he went home and said to his mother: "Why don't you hurry up and die? I promised to lament you very bitterly."

A man who looks forward to his mother's death will hardly be able to lament it bitterly.

Huai Nan Zi

瞎子和跛子

寇难至,躄者告盲者,盲者负而走,两人皆活。得其所能也。

——《淮南子》

THE BLIND MAN AND THE LAME MAN

A certain country was invaded by its enemy. When a lame man there told a blind man of this, the blind man carried the lame one on his back and they escaped together. They did this by making use of each other's strong points.

Huai Nan Zi

两只眼睛

昔有二人共评主者：

一人曰："好"，一人曰："丑"。

久而不决；二人各曰："尔可求人，吾目中则好丑分矣"。

士有定形，二人察之有得失，非苟相反，眼睛异耳。

—— 《万机论》

TWO PAIRS OF EYES

Two men were discussing the appearance of their master.

"How handsome he is!" said one.

"How ugly!" said the other.

They argued for a long time and no conclusion could be reached. Finally each said to the other, "Get someone else to look at him and he will tell you that I'm right!"

—One's features cannot be changed by other people's comments. That the two men should have different views is not because they want to oppose each other, but because each sees through his own eyes.

Wan Ji Lun

一个洞的"网"

语有之曰:"有鸟将来,张罗待之,得鸟者一目也。"

今为一目之罗,无时得鸟矣。

—— 《申鉴》

ONE-HOLE NETS

There is an old saying, "No matter how big a net one may spread, each bird is caught in a single hole."

Now a person was so fascinated by this witticism that he took a number of pieces of string and made separate loops of them by tying the ends together.

Consequently never once did he catch a bird with those "nets."

Shen Jian

杯弓蛇影

予之祖父郴，为汲令，以夏至日诣见主簿杜宣，赐酒。

时北壁上有悬赤弩，照于杯，形如蛇。宣畏恶之，然不敢不饮。其日，便得胸腹痛切，妨损饮食，大用羸露，攻，万端不为愈。复郴因事过至宣家窥视，问其变故。云："畏此蛇。蛇入腹中。"郴还听事，思惟良久。顾见悬弩，"必是也！"则使门下史将铃下待徐扶辇载宣，于故处设酒，杯中故复有蛇。因谓宣："此壁上弩影可，非有他怪。"

THE REFLECTION OF THE BOW

My grandfather, who was magistrate of the district of Chen, once invited his secretary, Du Xuan, to drink with him during the midsummer festival. A red bow which was hanging on the north wall cast a reflection in the cup just like a snake; but although Du Xuan was frightened he dared not refuse to drink. Then he had a severe pain in his stomach, and could not eat, so that he grew very thin. Though he tried all manner of drugs, he could find no cure.

Later my grandfather called on him on some business, and asked him how he had contracted this illness.

"Through fear of the snake which I swallowed, "Du Xuan told him.

After going home my grandfather thought this over, then turned and saw the bow, and understood what had happened. He sent a subordinate with a carriage to escort Du Xuan to his house, and set wine in the same place, so that once more a snake appeared in the cup.

"This is simply a reflection of that bow on the wall, " he told his secretary.

宣遂解。甚夷怿。由是瘳平。

——《风俗通》

At once Du Xuan felt better and, greatly relieved, recovered.

Traditional Topics (*Feng Su tong*)

白头猪

　　往时辽东有豕,生子白头,异而献之;
行至河东,见豕皆白,怀惭而还。

——《后汉书》

THE PIG WITH THE WHITE HEAD

Once in Liaodong a swineherd's sow farrowed a piglet with a white head, and thinking it a prodigy he decided to present it to the court. When he reached Hedong, however, he found that all the pigs there had white heads; so he went sheepishly home.

The Later Han History

神 鱼

会稽石亭埭,有大枫树,其中空朽,每雨水辄满溢。

有估客,载生鳢至此,聊放一头于朽树中,以为狡狯。

村民见之,以鱼鳢非树中之物,咸谓是神。乃依树起屋,宰牲祭祀,未尝虚日,因遂名鳢父庙。人有祈请及秽慢,则祸福立至。

后估客返,见其如此,即取作臛,于是遂绝。

—— 《异苑》

THE HOLY EEL

At Stone Pavilion Dam in Kuaiji there stands a great maple tree. The trunk has rotted and is hollow; so whenever it rains, a hole in the tree becomes filled with water. A merchant passing here with a load of eels put one eel in the rotten tree for fun.

Since eels do not grow on trees, when the villagers saw it they were sure it must be holy. They built a temple by the tree, slaughtered cattle to sacrifice every day, and called the place The Temple o Father Eel. They believed that those who prayed at the shrine would immediately have good fortune, while those who offended the god would be overtaken by calamity.

When the merchant came back this way and saw what had happened, he took the eel to make eel broth. And so it ceased being holy.

The Garden of Marvels (Yi Yuan)

159

刻凤凰

　　公输之刻凤凰也：冠距未成，翠羽未树，人见其身者谓之"鶵鵄"，见其首者名曰："鹒鹑"，皆訾其丑而笑其拙。

　　及凤之成，翠冠云耸，朱距电摇，锦身霞散，绮翮焱发，洩然一翥，翻翔云栋，三日而不集，然后赞其奇而称其巧。

——《刘子》

CARVING A PHOENIX

Gong Shu, the artisan, was carving a phoenix in wood.

As a start he sketched a rough outline of the bird on the block of wood.

Looking at the drawing, one said, "It looks more like an owl than a phoenix."

Another said, "It reminds me of an egret."

All laughed at the ugliness of the bird and the clumsiness of the artisan.

In due time, the phoenix appeared, with a crown like a sapphire, vermilion claws and a dazzling plumage. A touch on a hidden spring and it soared high up into the sky where it remained on wing among the clouds for three days and nights.

Those who had given voice to such idle opinions were now all praise for the wonderful skill of the artisan.

Liu Zi

博士买驴

博士买驴,书卷三纸,未有驴字。

—— 《颜氏家训》

A SCHOLAR BUYS A DONKEY

One day a learned scholar was buying a donkey on the market.

A deed had to be filled out recording the transaction.

The man who had sold the donkey watched the scholar writing sheet after sheet till three sheets were finished, but could not see the word "donkey." He urged the scholar to complete the deed.

"You only have to make it clear in the deed that the donkey has been paid for and that the liability is involved by either party. Why are you writing so much?" asked the seller in wonder.

"Don't be impatient, I'll soon come to the donkey, " was the reply.

Yan's Family Instructions

枣红马

　　王皓性迂缓。曾从齐文宣北伐,乘一赤马,平旦蒙霜,遂不复识,自言失马,虞候遍求不获。

　　须臾,日出,马体霜尽,依然系在前。方云:"我马尚在"。

——《北史》

"IT WAS HERE ALL THE TIME!"

Wang Hao was a slow-witted man. Once he accompanied the emperor of Qi to battle riding on a chestnut horse. During the night, it turned very cold. When morning came, the horse was coated with sleet. When he went out he could not find his horse, so he ordered a search for it, but in vain.

When the sun rose, the sleet melted and the horse reappeared.

"Oh, it was here all the time!" he said.

History of the Northern Dynasties

自寻死路

周定州刺史孙彦高,被突厥围城数十重,不敢诣所。文符须征发者,于小窗接入,锁州宅门。

及贼登垒,乃入匮中藏,令奴曰:"牢拿钥匙,贼来索,慎勿与。"

—— 《朝野佥载》

COWARDICE MAKES MEN INTO FOOLS

The city of Dingzhou was surrounded by the Tartar army. Sun Yangao, the prefect, was so frightened he no longer appeared at his official quarters, but shut himself in his private house and had the door bolted. Official documents were passed through a tiny window.

When he learned that the Tartars had scaled the ramparts, he hurried to hide himself in a large wooden chest, saying to his servant, "Lock it from the outside, keep the key and don't give it to the robbers when they ask for it!"

Chao Ye Xian Zai

167

丢了皮口袋

昔有愚人入京选，皮袋被贼盗去。

其人曰："贼偷我袋，将终不得我物也。"

或问其故？答曰："钥匙尚在我衣带上，彼将何物开之？"

——《朝野金载》

THE LOST BAG

There was once a fool who, on coming to the capital for the civil examination, discovered that he had lost his leather bag.

"Though a thief has stolen my bag, " he said calmly, "he won't be able to touch the contents."

Asked why, he said, "I still have the key, so what is he going to open the bag with?"

Chao Ye Xian Zai

开 井

　　凿井于路旁,用济路人之渴。一有堕之者,则罪凿井焉。

——《伸蒙子》

THE WELL

A well was sunk by the roadside. People in the habit of using the road who had not been able to find a drop of water to quench their thirst in the past found it very convenient.

After some time, however, a man going home one night fell into the well and was drowned. Then people began to blame the person who had chosen that site for the well.

Shen Meng Zi

鸩鸟和毒蛇

鸩与蛇相遇,鸩前而啄之。

蛇谓曰:"世人皆毒子矣,毒者恶名也,子所以有恶名者,以食我也,于不食我则无毒,不毒则恶名亡矣。"

鸩笑曰:"汝岂不毒于世人哉!指我为毒,是欺也。夫汝毒于世人者,有心啮人也,吾怨汝之啮人,所以食汝示刑也。世人审吾之能刑汝,故畜吾以防汝,又审汝之毒染吾毛羽肢体,故用杀人。吾之毒,汝之毒也。吾疾恶而蒙其名尔;然杀人者,人也,犹人持兵而杀人也。兵罪乎?人罪乎?则非吾之毒也明矣。世人所以蓄吾而不蓄汝,又明矣。吾无心毒人,而疾恶得名,为人所用,吾所为能全其身也。全身而甘恶名,非恶名矣。汝以有心之毒盱睢于草莽

172

THE FALCON AND THE ADDER

The falcon met an adder on the road and advanced to peck at it.

"Don't you peck me!" said the adder to the falcon. "People say you're poisonous. That's a bad thing to be called, and it's because you eat us. If you don't eat us you won't get our venom in you and people will no longer hate you."

"Quiet, you!" scoffed the falcon. "It's a lie to say I'm poisonous. It's you who bite men with malicious intent, and I'm eating you to punish you for your crimes. People keep me because they know I can bring you to account. They know too that my limbs and feathers are contaminated with your venom; that is why they use these as a means to poison others. But that's no concern of mine. It's like the weapon a man uses to kill someone. Is the weapon to blame? Or the man? I don't harm people wilfully, and I'm used as a weapon against wickedness. But as for you , you lurk in the grass , intent on harming

之间,伺人以自快。今遇我,天也,而欲诡
辩苟免卯邪?"

　　蛇不能答,鸩食之。

——《无能子》

people. Fate has ordained that you should come my way today. No sophistry can help you."

So saying, the falcon swallowed up the adder.

Wu Neng Zi

要钱不要命

永之氓，咸善游。一日水暴甚，有五六氓乘小船，绝湘水中济，船破皆游。其一氓尽力而不能寻常。

其侣曰："汝善游最也，今何后焉？"

曰："吾腰千钱重，是以后。"曰："何不去之？"

不应，摇其首。有顷，益怠。

已济者立岸上，呼且号曰："汝愚之甚，蔽之甚，身且死，何以货为？"

又摇其首，遂溺死。

—— 《柳河东集》

THE MAN WHO LIKED MONEY
BETTER THAN LIFE

In Yongzhou there were many good swimmers. One day, the river swelled suddenly. Braving the danger, about half a dozen people started across in a small boat. While they were still in midstream, the boat capsized. Whereupon, they started to swim. One, though using his arms vigorously, seemed to make small progress.

"You're a better swimmer than any of us, why are you lagging behind?" asked his companions.

"I have a thousand coins tied around my loin," said the man.

"Why don't you throw them away?" urged the others.

He made no answer, shaking his head, although he was clearly in difficulties.

The others reached the shore and shouted out to him: "Off with the coins, you fool! What's the use of the money to you when you are drowning?"

Still the man shook his head. In a few moments he was drowned.

Collected Works of Liu Zongyuan

黔驴技穷

　　黔无驴,有好事者,船载以入;至则无可用,放之山下。虎见之,庞然大物也,以为神;蔽林间窥之,稍出近之,慭慭然,莫相知。他日,驴一鸣,虎大骇远遁,以为且噬己也,甚恐;然往来视之,觉无异能者;益习其声,又近出前后,终不敢搏。稍近益狎,荡倚冲冒,驴不胜怒,蹄之。虎因喜,计之曰:"技止此耳!"因跳踉大㘎,断其喉,尽其肉,乃去。

——《柳河东集》

THE DONKEY OF GUIZHOU

There were no donkeys in Guizhou until an eccentric took one there by boat; but finding no use for it he set it loose in the hills. A tiger who saw this monstrous-looking beast thought it must be divine. It first surveyed the donkey from under cover, then ventured a little nearer, still keeping a respectful distance however.

One day the donkey brayed, and the tiger took fright and fled, for fear of being bitten. It was utterly terrified. But it came back for another look, and decided this creature was not so formidable after all. Then, growing used to the braying, it drew nearer, though it still dared not attack. Coming nearer still, it began to take liberties, shoving, jostling, and charging roughly, till the donkey lost its temper and kicked out.

"So that is all it can do!" thought the tiger, greatly pleased.

Then it leaped on the donkey and sank its teeth into it, severing its throat and devouring it before going on its way.

Collected Works of Liu Zongyuan

用骗术的猎人

　　鹿畏貙，貙畏虎，虎畏罴。罴之状，被
发人立，绝有力而甚害人焉！

　　楚之南有猎者，能吹竹为百兽之音，寂
寂持弓矢罌火而即之山为鹿鸣，以感其类，
伺其至，发火而射之。貙闻其鹿也，趋而
至，其人恐，因为虎骇之。貙走而虎至，愈
恐，则又为罴，虎亦亡去。罴闻而求其类，
至则人也，捽搏挽裂而食之。

　　今夫不善内而恃外者，未有不为罴之
食也！

—— 《柳河东集》

THE HUNTER WHO USED TRICKS

The deer is afraid of the wolf; the wolf of the tiger; and the tiger of the wild bear, the most ferocious and powerful of all animals, walking erect, with long hair hanging from its head.

In southern Chu there was a hunter who could blow a bamboo pipe to imitate the sounds of various animals. He used to lure the deer from their mountain fastness by mimicking their noise, and then shoot them down.

One day, he was at his tricks again. The wolf, hearing the pipe, thought it was deer and came. The hunter was frightened, so he imitated the roar of a tiger. Off went the wolf, but a tiger appeared. Terror-stricken, the hunter made the sound of the bear. The tiger made off. The bear, hearing the noise, thought it was one of its kind and came. Finding it to be a man, it tore him limb from limb and ate him up.

—If a man refuses to improve his inner self, and depends on external forces, he can hardly avoid a similar fate to that of the hunter.

Collected Works of Liu Zongyuan

糊涂的小鹿

　　临江之人，畋得麋麑，畜之。入行，群犬垂涎，扬尾皆来，其人怒怛之。自是日抱就犬习示之使勿动，稍使与之戏。积久，犬皆如人意。麋麑稍大，忘己之麋也，以为犬良我友，抵触偃仆，益狎。犬畏主人，与之俯仰甚善，然时啖其舌。

　　三年麋出门，见外犬在道甚众，走欲与为戏。外犬见而喜且怒，共杀食之，狼藉道上，麋至死不悟。

——《柳河东集》

THE SILLY FAWN

A man in Linjiang captured a fawn. When it was brought home, the dogs came licking their chops and wagging their tails. The man angrily drove them off. Afterwards, he took the fawn among the dogs, warning them to keep their peace, and making them frolic with it. In time, the dogs learned their lesson. As the fawn grew, it forgot it was a deer and regarded the dogs as its friends, with whom it could gambol and play. The dogs, fearing their master, had to suppress their natural desires and fraternize with it.

One day after three years, the deer went outside the gate. There were many strange dogs in the street, so it went up and tried to play with them. The dogs were surprised, but being glad to see a meal come their way, fell upon it and killed it. As it was breathing its last, the deer was at a loss to understand why it had come to such an untimely end.

Collected Works of Liu Zongyuan

老规矩

　　杨叔贤郎中异，眉州人，言顷有太守初视事，人排乐。乐人口号云："为报吏民须庆贺，灾星移去福星来!"守大喜，问口号谁撰，优人答曰："本州自来旧例，止此一首。"

—— 《湘山野录》

OLD CUSTOM

A newly-appointed prefect was giving a grand banquet for the local gentry with many musicians to entertain the party. In the midst of the revelry, a singer intoned: "Out with the old, in with the new; out with the evil star, in with the lucky star!"

The prefect was highly flattered.

"Who composed that?" he asked.

"It is an old custom in our town to sing this when a new prefect arrives. It is the only couplet I know, " replied the singer.

Xiang Shan Ye Lu

雁奴

雁奴,雁之最小者,性尤机警。每群雁夜宿,雁奴独不瞑,为之伺察。或微闻人声,必先号鸣,群雁则杂然相呼引去。后乡人益巧设诡计,以中雁奴之欲。于是先视陂薮雁所常处者,阴布大网,多穿土穴于其傍。日未入,人各持束缊并匿穴中,须其夜艾;则爇火穴外,雁奴先警,急灭其火。群雁惊视无见,复就栖焉。于是三爇三灭,雁奴三叫,众雁三惊;已而无所见,则众雁谓奴之无验也,互啄迭击之,又就栖然。少选,火复举,雁奴畏众击,不敢鸣。乡人闻其无声,乃举网张之,率十获五。

——《景文集》

THE WILD GOOSE SENTRY

The smallest and the most alert of a flock of wild geese is often chosen to keep vigil for the others during the night. At the slightest untoward sound it raises the alarm and the flock start from their sleep and make off.

So some wild goose hunters once devised a scheme to outwit the sentry. First they marked the haunt of the flock, spread an enormous net there and hid themselves in holes dug nearby.

As night fell, the flock descended and went to sleep. The hunters lit a torch. As soon as the sentry gave the warning, they extinguished the torch. The flock, startled to their feet, found it all quiet and went back to sleep. The trick was repeated three times. On the third occasion the flock decided the sentry was inefficient and pecked him by way of chastisement. Then they went back to sleep.

After some time, the hunters again lit the torch. This time the sentry remained silent. Hearing no stir among the flock, the hunters drew in the net, bagging more than half the birds.

Work of Jing Wen

另开一个大池子

　　王荆公好言利,有小人诏曰:"决梁山泊八百里水以为田,其利大矣。"

　　荆公喜甚,徐曰:"决水何地可容?"

　　刘贡父曰:"自其旁别凿八百里泊,则可容矣。"

　　荆公笑而止。

——《邵氏见闻录》

A NEW LAKE FOR AN OLD

Wang Anshi, prime minister of the Song Dynasty, was fond of public utility projects. A man who wanted to get into his good graces offered a proposition. "Drain Liangshanbo Lake, and you will have eight hundred square *li* of fertile land, " said the man.

Wang Anshi was elated, then he asked, "Where shall the water go?"

"Dig another lake of the same size beside it and the question is solved, " said Liu Kongfu.

Wang Anshi laughed and called the matter off.

The Records of Shao

古书换古铜

　　有一士人，尽掊其家所有，约百余千，买书将以入京。至中涂，遇一士人，取其书目阅之，爱其书而贫不能得，家有数古铜器将以货之，而鬻书者雅有好古器之癖，一见喜甚。乃曰："无庸货也，我将与汝估其直而两易之"。于是尽所随行之书换数十铜器。

　　亟返其家，其妻方讶夫之回，疾视其行李，但见二三布囊磊块然，铿铿有声。问得其实，乃詈其夫曰："你换得他这个，几时近

ANCIENT BOOKS FOR
ANCIENT BRONZE

A scholar, hard-pressed for money, listed a few hundred of his books, packed them up, and set out for the capital, intending to sell them. On his way he met another scholar who looked at his list and wanted to buy them. But he could not afford the price. He happened to have a few pieces of ancient bronze at home which he intended to sell for rice. So he took the other to see them. The one who wanted to sell his books was a great admirer of bronze, and was delighted with these specimens.

"No need to sell them, " he told the other. "We can weigh the price of the books against the bronze and see if we can't do an exchange." The outcome was that he deposited his books with the other and left with a load of bronze.

When he reached home, his wife was surprised to see him back so soon. Looking quickly at his bags, she found they were full of some hard objects which clanged when shifted about. When she heard the story, she began to scold.

"You fool!" she exclaimed. "What do you want these things for when we have no rice in the house?"

得饭吃?"其人曰:"他换得我那个也,则几时近得饭吃?"

——《道山清话》

192

"He's in the same fix, " replied the husband, cheerfully. "With the books he has from me, he won't have any rice to eat for some time either!"

Dao Shan Qing Hua

船主的如意算盘

艾子见有人徒行，自吕良托舟人以趋彭门者，持五十钱遗舟师。师曰："凡无赍而独载者人百金。汝尚少半，汝当自此为我牵去彭门，可折半直也。"

——《艾子杂说》

THE BOAT-OWNER'S BRIGHT IDEA

Once I saw a man travelling on foot at Lüliang. He saw a boat, and offered the boat-owner fifty coins to take him to Pengmen.

"According to the usual rates," said the boat-owner, "a passenger making a trip without cargo should pay a hundred coins. Now you're offering half, that's not enough. But since I have to pay fifty coins for a man to tow my boat, I'll take you for fifty if you agree to tow my boat to Pengmen!"

Miscellanea of Ai Zi

瞎子问太阳

生而眇者不识日,问之有目者。

或者之曰:"日之状如铜盘。"扣盘而得其声,他曰,闻钟以为日也。

或告之曰:"日之光为烛。"扪烛而得其形,他曰,揣籥以为日也。

日之与钟籥亦远而眇者不知其异,以其未尝见而求之人也。

——《苏轼文集》

WHAT DOES THE SUN LOOK LIKE?

A man who was born blind wanted to know what the sun looked like, so he asked others to describe it.

"It looks like this, like a bronze disc, " said one, rapping a gong as he spoke. Some time later, when the blind man heard a gong, he said, "Isn't that the sun?"

Another told him, "The sun has light like this candle, " and let him feel the candle. Some time later, the blind man picked up a flute and exclaimed, "Ah! This is surely the sun."

A sun is a far cry from a gong or a flute, but the blind cannot make out the difference because they cannot see and have to ask others.

Collected Essays of Su Shi

斗牛图

　　蜀中有杜处士,好书画,所宝以百数。有戴嵩牛一轴,尤所爱,锦囊玉轴,常以自随。

　　一日曝书画。而一牧童见之,拊掌大笑,曰:"此画斗牛也,牛斗力在角,尾搐入两股间,今乃掉尾而斗,谬矣!"处士笑而然之。

——《东坡志林》

THE FIGHTING OXEN

A great artist painted a picture of two oxen fighting.

Everybody praised it.

"Look! How spirited they look, like live ones."

The artist swelled with pride. He had the painting mounted on precious silk hung from jade rods, and put it away in a cedar chest. Rarely would he show it to anyone except those who could appreciate fine work.

One day he took the painting from the chest, unrolled it, and hung it in the sun, as a precaution against bookworms.

Just then a cowherd entered the courtyard, stood before the picture and smiled broadly.

"When oxen fight and but with their horns, " said the boy, "they keep their tails tucked between their rumps. Now in this picture, they're flicking their tails about. I' ve never seen oxen fighting like that before."

The great painter had no answer to this.

Dong Po Zhi Lin

米从哪里来

蔡京诸孙,长生膏粱,不知稼穑。

一日,京戏问之曰:"汝曹日啖饭,试为我言米从何处出?"

其一对曰:"从白子里出"。京大笑。

其一旁应曰:"不是,我见在席子里出。"盖京师运米以席囊盛之,故云。

—— 《独醒杂志》

200

WHENCE COMES RICE?

The grandsons of Cai Jing, the notorious prime minister, who grew up in riches, could not tell wheat from rice.

One day, while having a meal, Cai Jing said, "You eat rice every day. Do you know where it comes from?"

"From the mortar, " one hazarded. Cai Jing laughed.

"No, it doesn't!" said the other. "It comes from rush-mats. I saw it!" In those days rice was transported into the capital in bags made of rush-mats, hence the conclusion.

Du Xing Za Zhi

囫囵吞枣

客有曰："梨益齿而损脾，枣益脾而损齿。"

一呆子方思久之曰："我食梨则嚼而不咽，不能伤我之脾；我食枣则吞而不嚼，不能伤我之齿。"

—— 《湛渊静语》

SWALLOWING A DATE WHOLE

A fool once heard someone say that pears were good for the teeth but harmful to the spleen, and that dates were good for the spleen but harmful to the teeth. After pondering the matter a considerable while, he said:

"From now on, when I eat a pear, I will only chew and not swallow it. And when I eat a date, I will swallow it whole."

Zhan Yuan Jing Yu

大善士

昔有人得一鳖,欲烹而食之,不忍当杀生之名,乃炽火使釜自沸,横筷为桥,与鳖约曰:"能渡此则活汝。"

鳖知主人以计取之,勉力爬沙,仅能一渡。

主人曰:"汝能渡桥甚善,更为渡一遭。"

—— 《程史》

THE COMPASSIONATE MAN

A compassionate man once caught a turtle. He wanted to make it into soup, but unwilling to be accused of taking life, he boild a panful of water and, placing a rod over the pan, said to the turtle, "If you can get across the pan, I will set you free."

The turtle was in no doubt as to the intentions of the man. But he did not want to die. So, summoning up all his will, he accomplished the impossible.

"Well done!" said the man. "But please try it again!"

Cheng Shi

中山狼

　　赵简子大猎于中山，有狼当道，驱车逐之。时东郭先生，将北适中山以干仕，策蹇驴，囊图书，夙行失道。狼奄至，引首顾曰："先生岂有志于济物哉？何不使我早处囊中，以苟延残喘乎？异时倘得脱颖而出，先生之恩，生死而肉骨也。"先生及出图书空囊橐，徐徐焉实狼其中。已而简子至，求狼弗得，回车就道。狼度简子之去远，而作声囊中曰："先生可留意矣，出我囊。"先生举手出狼，狼咆哮谓先生曰："适为虞人逐，其来甚速，幸先生生我，我饿甚，馁不得食，亦终必亡而已，又何吝一躯啖我，而全微命乎！"遂鼓吻奋爪以向先生。先生仓卒以手搏之，还望老子杖藜而来，先生且喜且愕，

THE WOLF OF THE
ZHONGSHAN MOUNTAIN

There once lived a scholar by the name of Dongguo, who was known for his compassion.

One day, he was riding along on a donkey on his way to Zhongshan, when he saw a group of hunters. A little while later a wolf came running up to him in great fright. "Kind-hearted master, " it begged. "Please let me get into your bag and hide for a while. If ever I should emerge alive from this crisis, I will for ever remember your kindness."

Hearing this, the master emptied his bag of books, pushed the wolf inside, and packed the books in around him.

Presently the hunters arrived. Not finding the wolf, they went away.

The wolf then asked Master Dongguo to let him out of the bag, which the master did.

Thereupon the wolf bared his fangs and said, "I was being chased by wicked men and I am grateful to you for saving my life. Now I am starving and will die unless I have something to eat. You'll have to let me eat you, if you want to save me." So saying, it fell upon the master, catching him completely by surprise. The master was defending himself as best he could when, to his intense relief, he saw an old man approaching. Extricat-

舍狼而前,拜跪啼泣,致辞曰:"乞丈人一言而生。"丈人问故,先生曰:"是狼为虞人所窘,求救于我,我实生之,今反欲噬我,敢乞一言而生。"狼曰:"初先生救我时,束缚我足,闭我囊中,压以诗书,我鞠躬不敢息,又蔓词以说简子,其意盖将死我于囊,而独窃其利也,吾安可不噬。"丈人曰:"是皆不足以执信也!试再囊之,吾观其状,果困苦否。"狼欣然从之。丈人附耳谓先生曰:"有匕首否?"先生曰:"有。"于是出匕,丈人目先生使引匕刺狼,先生曰:"不害狼乎!"丈人笑曰:"禽兽负恩为是,而犹不忍杀,子固仁者,然愚亦甚矣。"遂举手助先生操刀,共殪狼,弃道上而去。

—— 《中山狼传》

ing himself for a moment, he ran up to the old man, begging him to save him.

"Why, what's up?" asked the old man.

"That wolf had the hunters on his trail and asked me to help him, " said the master. "I saved his life. But now he wants to eat me. Please talk to him and tell him he is in the wrong."

"When the master hid me away, "said the wolf, "he bound my feet, pushed me into the bag and pressed the books in after me. I curled up as tightly as I could, but I couldn't breathe. Then he had a long conversation with the hunters, intending that I should suffocate in the bag. Why should I not eat him?"

"I think perhaps you are exaggerating, "said the old man. "Show me what happened, and let me see if you really suffered as much as you say you did."

The wolf gladly complied and crawled into the bag.

"Do you have a dagger?" the old man whispered to Master Dongguo.

The master produced one. Whereupon the old man signed to him to knife the wolf.

"Won't it hurt him!" demurred the master.

The old man laughed. "This is a most ungrateful beast, yet you don't have the heart to kill it. You are indeed a man of compassion, but you are also very foolish!"

So he helped Master Dongguo to slay the wolf.

Story of the Wolf of the Zhongshan Mountain

奉 承

鲁有迂滑二叟,踞石而谈。

迂叟曰:"余有百金,以十之二予若,若趋承予否?"

滑叟曰:"物不均,不得趋承!"

"然则平分之?"

曰:"物之均,不得趋承!"

"然则全予乎?"

曰:"物全归,不用趋承。"

—— 《艾子外语》

210

WILL YOU FLATTER ME?

A rich man and a poor man were talking together.

"I have a hundred ounces of gold, " said the rich man. "If I give you twenty, will you flatter me?"

"It would not be fairly shared, so how could I flatter you?"

"Suppose I give you half, would you flatter me then?"

"We would be equal. I would not flatter you."

"And if I give you all the gold, how then?"

"If I had all the gold, I would have no need to flatter you."

Ai Zi Wai Yu

两个射雁的人

昔人有睹雁翔者,将授弓射之,曰:"获则烹。"其弟争曰:"舒雁烹宜,翔雁燔宜。"竞斗而讼于社伯,社伯请剖雁,烹燔半焉。已而索雁,则凌空远矣。

—— 《贤奕编》

TWO WAYS OF COOKING THE GOOSE

A man saw a wild goose flying in the sky. Fitting an arrow to his bow, he said, "If I can bring it down, we will stew it."

"No, it would be better to roast it," said his younger brother.

Their argument reached a deadlock. Finally they went to a senior member of their clan who settled the matter by suggesting a half-and-half treatment. But when they came out to look for the wild goose again, it was nowhere to be seen.

Xian Yi Pian

213

医驼背

　　昔有医人，自媒能治背驼，曰："如弓者、为虾者、如曲环者，延吾治，可朝治而夕如矢。"一人信焉，而使治驼。乃索板二片，以一置地下，卧驼者其上，又以一压焉，而即踩焉，驼者随直，亦复随死。

　　其子欲鸣诸官，医人曰："我业治驼，但管人直，那管人死。"

—— 《雪涛小说》

TREATING HUNCHBACKS

There was once a charlatan who claimed he could cure deformities of the spine. "Whether your back is like a bow, a shrimp, a ring, or whatever you please, come to me and I'll straighten it in no time."

One hunchback was credulous enough to take his words at their face value and came to him for treatment. The charlatan made him lie prone on a plank, put another on his hump, then jumped up and down on it with all his might. The hump was straightened, but the man died.

The man's son wanted to sue him, but the charlatan said, "My job is to straighten his hump. Whether or not he dies, has nothing to do with me."

Stories by Xue Tao

做 梦

尝闻一青衿,生性狡,能以谲计诳人。学博持教甚严,诸生稍或犯规,必遣人执之,扑无赦。

一日,此生适有犯,学博追执甚急,坐彝伦堂盛怒待之。

已而生至,长跪地下,不言他事,但曰:"弟子偶得千金,方在处置,故未见迟耳。"

博士闻生得金多,辄霁怒,问之曰:"尔金从何处来?"

曰:"得诸地中。"

又问:"尔欲作何处置?"

生答曰:"弟子故贫,无资业,今与妻计:以五百金市田,二百金市宅,百金置器,买童妾,止剩百金,以其半市书,将发愤从事焉,而以其半致馈先生,酬平日教育,完矣。"

THE DREAM

There was once a proctor who was very strict with his students. One day, a student committed a breach of discipline. Pulling a long face, the proctor sent for the offender, and sat himself in a chair to await his arrival. The student finally appeared, and, kneeling before the proctor, said, "I meant to come earlier. But the fact is I have just found a thousand ounces of gold and I've had a hard time deciding how to dispose of it."

The proctor melted a little when he heard about the gold. "Where did you find it?" He asked.

"Buried under the ground!"

"And what are you going to do with it?" asked the proctor again.

"I was a poor man, sir, " answreed the student. "I have talked it over with my wife and we agreed to put aside 500 ounces to buy land, 200 for a house, 100 to buy furniture and another hundred to buy maidservants and pages. Then we'll use one half of the last hundred to buy books, for from now on I must study hard, and the other half I will make as a small present to you for the pains you took in educating me."

博士曰:"有是哉,不佞何以当之!"

遂呼使考治具,甚丰洁,延生坐觞之,谈笑欢洽,皆异平日。饮半酣,博士问生曰:"尔适匆匆来,亦曾收金箧中扃钥耶?"

生起应曰:"弟子布置此金甫定,为荆妻转身触弟子,醒已失金所在,安用箧?"

博士遽然曰:"尔所言金,梦耶?"

生答曰:"固梦耳。"

博士不怿,然业与欢洽,不能复怒,徐曰:"尔自雅情,梦中得金,就不忘先生,况实得耶?"更一再觞出之。

——《雪涛小说》

"Ah! Is that so! I don't think I have done enough to deserve so precious a gift, " said the proctor.

So saying, he ordered his cook to prepare a sumptuous dinner to which he invited the student. They had a happy time, talking and laughing and toasting each other 's health. Just as they were getting tipsy, the proctor had a sudden thought.

"You came away in a hurry, "he said. "Did you remember to lock the gold away in a cabinet before you came?"

The student rose to his feet. "Sir, I had just finished planning how to use the money when my wife rolled against me, and I opened my eyes to find the gold was gone. So what's the use of the cabinet?"

"So all this you've been talking about is only a dream?"gasped the proctor.

"Indeed, yes, " answered the student.

The proctor was angry, but since he had been so hospitable to the student, it would have seemed churlish to lose his temper with him now, so he contented himself with saying, "I can see you keep me in mind even when you are dreaming. Surely you won't forget me when you really have the gold?"

And he urged him to more drinks before he let him go.

Stories by Xue Tao

只是没有糟

　　余郡西三十里，有河洑山。山隈有王婆庙，不知何代人。父老相传，此婆酿酒为业。一道士往来其家，每索酒，辄予饮，累数百壶不酬值，婆不与较。一日道士谓婆曰："予饮若酒，无钱相值，请为若掘井。"井成，泉涌出，皆醇酒。道士曰："此以偿耳！"遂去。婆不复酿酒，但持井所出泉应酤者，比宿酿更佳，酤者踵至逾三年，得钱几数万，家遂富。前道士忽又至，婆深谢之。道士问曰："酒好否？"答曰："好倒好，只猪无糟耳！"道士笑题其壁曰："天高不算高，人

NO DREGS FOR THE SWINE

Thirty *li* west of my prefecture lies Hefu Mountain, in whose shelter nestles a temple dedicated to one Wang Po (Old Dame Wang). Nobody knows when this old woman lived. A story has it that she made a living by selling wine and that there was a Taoist priest who often came to her shop and drank wine without paying her. But the old woman did not seem to mind. One day, the priest said to her, "I have never paid you for any of the wine I have drunk, but I will sink a well for you." So the priest sank the well and it proved to contain the mellowest of wine. "This is my payment!" said the priest, and was gone.

The old woman no longer brewed her own wine but sold that from the well to the customers, who found it better than any they had ever tasted. Drinkers crowded her shop, and in three years she became very rich.

One day, the priest came again. The old woman thanked him.

"Is the wine good?" asked the priest.

"Very good, "answered the old woman. "Only there are no dregs for the swine!"

The priest laughed and wrote on the wall the following lines:

High is the sky,
But higher is human desire.

221

心第一高,井水做酒卖,还道猪无糟。"题讫
去,自是井不复出酒矣。

—— 《雪涛小说》

Well water she sells as wine,
Yet complains for lack of dregs for her swine!

Then the priest went away and the well gave no more wine.

Stories by Xue Tao

不认输

楚人有生而不识姜者,曰:"此从树上结成。"

或曰:"从土里生成。"

其人固执已见,曰:"请与予以十人为质,以所乘驴为赌。"

已而遍口十人,皆曰:"土里出也。"

其人哑然失色,曰:"驴则付汝,姜还树生。"

—— 《雪涛小说》

THE MAN WHO WOULD NOT
ADMIT HIS MISTAKE

In the state of Chu lived a man who did not know where ginger grew. He thought it grew on trees.

Someone told him it grew in the ground.

He could not believe this was true, and said, "I will lay a bet with you with my donkey. Let us ask ten people; if they all say it grows in the ground, the donkey is yours!"

They asked ten men who all said that it grew in the ground.

"Take the donkey!" said the man. "But, all the same, I know ginger grows on trees!"

Stories by Xue Tao

与我无关

又有医者,自称善外科。一裨将阵回,中流矢,深入膜内延使治。

乃持并州剪匕去矢管,跪而请谢。

裨将曰:"簇在膜内者须亟治。"

医曰:"此内科事,不意并责我。"

——《雪涛小说》

NOTHING TO DO WITH ME

A surgeon once boasted about his ability. A soldier, returning from battle with an arrow penetrating his leg, came to him for treatment.

The surgeon took a pair of sharp scissors and cut off the stem of the arrow close to the flesh, then asked for pay.

"But you haven't taken out the head of the arrow, " complained the soldier.

"That's an internal matter. That's a physician's business, not mine, " was the reply.

Stories by Xue Tao

耐　性

　　一仕官将之官,其厚友送之,嘱曰:"公居官无他难,只要耐烦。"仕者唯唯。

　　已而再嘱,三嘱,犹唯唯,及于四五,其人忿然怒曰:"君以我为呆子乎? 只此二字,奈何言之数四?"

　　厚友曰:"我才多说两次,尔遂发恼,辄为能耐烦可乎?"

—— 《雪涛小说》

PATIENCE

A man was going to take up an official post. A close friend came to see him off. "One thing you must remember when you become an official, " he said, " is that you must always be patient."

The man replied that he would. His friend then repeated his advice three times, and three times the man nodded in assent. When for the fourth time his friend repeated his counsel, the man became angry and said, "Do you take me for an idiot? Why do you repeat such a simple thing over and over again?"

His friend sighed. "It is not easy to be patient, see!" he said. "I have only said that a few times, and here you are already impatient."

Stories by Xue Tao

发　誓

　　有官人性贪,而示人以廉。初仕,向神发誓曰:"左手要钱,烂了左手;右手要钱,烂了右手。"

　　久之,有以百金行贿者,欲受之而疑前誓。左右为解曰:"请以此金纳官人袖中,便烂也只烂了袖子。"

　　官人然其言,辄纳之。

——《雪涛小书》

HONESTY

A corrupt official wanted to show that he was pure and honest. So, before assuming office, he took an oath in public, saying, "If my right hand accepts bribes, let it fester; if my left hand accepts bribes, let it fester, too."

After some time, a person offered him a hundred taels of silver as a bribe. He wanted to accept but feared that the oath might take effect.

To help him out of his quandary, the runner said, "Why not place the money in Your Honour's sleeve so that it, and it only, will rot, if rot it must!"

The official thought it was a sound idea and accepted the money.

Notes of Xue Tao

将军的错觉

一阃师,寒天夜宴,炽炭烧烛,引满浮白,酒后耳热,叹曰:"今年天气不正,当寒而暖。"

兵卒在旁跪禀曰:"较似小人们立处,天气觉正。"

—— 《雪涛小书》

ABNORMAL WEATHER

A general was drinking in the camp in a cold winter 's night. Candles were lighted and coal was burning well in the stove. After a few bowlfuls of wine, beads of sweat appeared on his forehead.

"Extraordinary weather we're having this year!" said the general. "When it should be cold, it's warm."

His words were heard by his orderly, who was standing outside in the cold. Entering the tent, he knelt respectfully before the general and said, "The weather seems normal enough where your servant was standing, sir."

Notes of Xue Tao

过手便酸

昔苏秦父母诞辰,伯子捧觞称寿! 叹曰:"好佳酿。"及季子亦捧觞称寿,骂曰:"酸酒"。

季子妻乃从伯姆借酒一觞,复骂曰:"酸酒。"

季子妻曰:"这是伯姆家借来的。"

翁叱之曰:"你这不行时的人,过手便酸。"

—— 《雪涛小书》

SOUR WINE

Su Qin had not been successful in his quest for an official post. One day a feast was held to celebrate his father's birthday.

When Su Qin's elder brother presented a cup of wine to the old man, he exclaimed on its excellence. But when Su Qin pressented a cup, his father pulled a wry face, and said, "Oh, how sour!"

Su Qin's wife thought perhaps the wine was really sour, so she borrowed some wine from the elder brother. But when she presented it, the old man still declared it was sour.

"This is the same wine that Su Qin's elder brother gave you, "she said.

"You luckless people! Even sweet wine turns sour when you touch it, " scolded the old man.

Notes of Xue Tao

对老虎发命令

杨叔贤为荆州幕时,虎伤人。杨就穴磨崖刻戒虎文,其略曰:"咄乎尔彪,出境潜游。"

后知郁林,致书知事赵定基,托拓戒虎文数本。云:"岭南俗庸犷,欲以此化之。"赵遣人打碑。次日耆申:"磨岩下大虫咬杀打碑匠二人。"赵乃以状寄答。

—— 《宋稗类抄》

ISSUING AN ORDER TO THE TIGERS

When Yang Shuxian was in office in Jingzhou, the tigers there were a scourge to the people. So Yang had an edict engraved on a big rock on a nearby mountain, ordering the tigers to leave the place.

Later, when he was transferred to Yulin, he found the people there very unruly. Thinking to issue to a similar edict, ordering them to be law-abiding, he wrote to the magistrate of Jingzhou asking for some rubbings to be taken of his edict to the tigers. When the magistrate sent some men to the mountain, they were killed by tigers while trying to take the rubbings.

The magistrate had to relate the tragedy in his reply to Yang.

Song Bai Lei Chao

神像和好人

　　乡村路口,有一神庙,乃是木雕之像。一人行路,因遇水沟,就将此神放倒,踏着过水。后有一人看见,心内不忍,将神扶在座上。

　　此神说他不供香火,登时就降他头痛之灾。

　　判官小鬼都禀道:"踏着大王过水的倒没事,扶起来的倒降灾,何也?"

　　这神说:"你不知道,只是善人好欺负。"

——《笑赞》

A GOOD MAN IS EASY TO BULLY

In the temple by the roadside of a village there was a wooden image of a deity. A man passing by found a ditch across his path, so he pulled down the image and placed it over the ditch as a bridge. Another passer-by saw the figure on the ground and, feeling sorry for it, restored it to its place. But the image took umbrage because he had offered no sacrifice to it, and placed a curse on him, causing him to suffer a bad headache.

The spirits of the kingdom of the underworld were non-plussed. "You let the one who trod on you go free, but punished the one who helped you up. Why?"

"You don't understand, " said the deity. "It is so easy to bully a good man."

Xiao Zan (*In Praise of Laughter*)

笑的一定不错

　　瞽者与人同坐。人有所见而笑，瞽者亦笑。或问汝何所见而笑？瞽答曰："诸君所笑，定然不差，难道是骗我的。"

——《笑赞》

LAUGH WITH OTHERS

A blind man was in the company of others. When his companions saw something funny, they laughed. The blind man laughed, too.

When they asked him why he was laughing, the blind man replied, "Since you laugh, there must be something worth laughing at. Can you be cheating me there?"

Xiao Zan

矮 凳

　　家有一坐头，绝低矮，迂公每坐，必取瓦片支其四足。后不胜烦，忽思得策，呼侍者，移置楼上坐。

　　及坐时，低为故，乃曰："人言楼高，浪得名耳。"

——《雅谑》

THE LOW STOOL

Yu Gong had a very low stool. When he wanted to sit on it, he always placed bricks under each leg. Later he found it very troublesome and hit upon an idea. He ordered a servant to take it upstairs. But when he sat on it again, he found it just as low.

"Well, people say it's higher upstairs, but I don't find it so!" he said.

Ya Nüe (***Merry Jokes***)

铁杵磨针

　　李白少读书，未成，弃去。道逢老妪磨杵，白问其故。曰："欲作针。"白感其言。遂卒业。

——《潜确类书》

GRINDING AN IRON
PESTLE INTO A NEEDLE

A schoolboy was playing truant in the street when he saw an old woman grinding an iron pestle on a stone.

Being curious, he asked her what she was doing.

"I am gonig to grind it into a needle to sew cloth with, " answered the old woman.

The child laughed. "But this is such a big pestle, how can you hope to grind it down to a needle?"

"It doesn't matter, " replied the old woman. "Today I grind it, tomorrow I'll grind it again, and the day after tomorrow again. The pestle will get smaller every day, and one day it will be a needle."

The child saw the point and went to school.

Qian Que Lei Shu

翠 鸟

　　翠鸟先高作巢以避患。及生子,爱之,恐坠,稍下作巢。予长羽毛,复益爱之,又更下巢,而人遂得而取之矣。

—— 《谭概》

THE KINGFISHER

The kingfisher is a timid bird. It always builds its nest high up in the tree as a protection against danger. When the fledglings hatch, it is so apprehensive for fear they should fall that it builds the nest lower down. When their feathers begin to appear, it becomes even more apprehensive and builds the nest still lower, so low that anybody can now catch them.

Tan Gai

猩　猩

　　猩猩知往而不知来。山谷间,常数十为群。里人以酒并糟设于路侧,织草为屐,更相连结。猩猩见酒及屐,知里人设张,则知张者祖先姓字,乃呼名云,奴欲张我,舍而去。后自再三,相谓曰:"试共尝酒。"及饮其味,逮乎醉。因取屐着之而踬。乃为人擒,无遗者。

——《谭概》

BABOONS

In the valleys in the south there are savage baboons which always go in groups. The local people, knowing their ways, place wine dregs by the roadside, and a string of straw sandals across the road. On seeing the wine and sandals, the baboons set up a loud clamour and turn tail. But they have already caught the scent of the wine. Cautiously, they begin to edge back, then scampering away and retracing their steps. Finally they decide to try a few mouthfuls. They drink the wine and get drunk, put on the sandals and trip and fall. Then the people come up and catch them.

Tan Gai

半日闲

有贵人游僧舍,酒甜,诵唐人诗云:"因过竹院逢僧话,又得浮生半日闲"。僧闻而笑之。贵人问僧何笑?僧曰:"尊官得半日闲,老僧却忙了三日。"

—— 《谭概》

A MOMENT OF IDLENESS

A high official paid a visit to a monastery. The monk in charge, having been notified of this previously, had made meticulous preparations for this occasion. After several drinks, the official recited a Tang poem:

Passing by the monastery I drop in to have a chat with the monk;
Out of this busy life a moment of idleness I enjoy.

The monk laughed. When asked why he laughed, he replied, "Your Worship has enjoyed a moment of idleness, but I've been busy for three days."

Tan Gai

墨 鱼

　　海中乌鲗鱼,有八足,能集攒口,缩口藏腹,腹含墨,值渔艇至,即喷墨以自蔽。渔视水黑,辄取网获之。

——《谭概》

THE CUTTLEFISH

The cuttlefish has four pairs of legs which it can draw into its beak, and it can hide its beak under its belly. As an added precaution against danger, it emits a jet of ink to screen itself and it does this when it meets a fishing boat. Whereupon the fisherman casts his net on the inky spot and takes it out of the water.

Tan Gai

我想要你的手指

一贫士遇故人于途；故人已得仙术矣。相劳苦中，因指道旁一砖成赤金赠之。士嫌其少，更指一大石狮为赠，士嫌未已。

仙曰：“汝欲如何？”

士曰：“愿乞公此指！”

—— 《笑府》

I WANT YOUR FINGER

A poor man one day met an old friend who had become an immortal. After hearing his freind complain of his poverty, the imortal pointed his finger at a brick by the roadside, which immediately turned into a gold ingot. He presented it to his friend. When the man was not satisfied with this, he gave him a big gold lion. But the man was still not appeased.

"What more do you want?" asked his immortal friend.

"I want your finger!" was the reply.

Xiao Fu

爱惜驴子

某翁富而吝,善权子母,责负无虚日。后以年且老,难于途,遂买一驴代步。顾爱惜甚至,非甚困惫,未尝肯据鞍。驴出翁胯下者,步不过数四。

值天暑,有所索于远道,不得已,与驴俱中道,翁喘,乃跨驴,驰二三里;驴不习骑,亦喘,翁惊亟下,解其鞍。驴以为息己也,望故道逸归。翁急遽呼驴,驴走不顾,追之弗及也;大惧驴亡,又吝于弃鞍,因负鞍趋归家,亟问驴在否?其子曰:"驴在。"

ALL FOR THE LOVE OF A DONKEY

A rich old miser made much money by giving high-interest loans. When he became too old to walk, he bought a donkey. But he became so fond of the animal that he would not ride it except when he was extremely tried.

One day it was hot and sultry. The old man had to make a long journey, so he took the donkey with him. After walking some distance, he became short of breath and mounted the donkey. After doing two or three *li*, the donkey also breathed hard, for it was not used to being ridden. The old man dismounted in alarm and unsaddled the animal. Whereupon the donkey, thinking it was turned loose, took to its heels and bolted for home, ignoring the old man's shouts. In vain did he try to overtake it. Fearing the donkey might get lost and not wishing to lose the saddle, he hurried home, shouldering the saddle.

As soon as he reached home, he asked whether the donkey had returned. When his son answered that it

翁乃复喜,徐释鞍,始觉足顿而背裂也,又伤于暑,病逾月乃瘥。

——《耳食录》

had, he cheered up. Then the exertion and the heat began to tell. The old man fell sick and took to his bed for
over a month.

Er Shi Lu (*Stories from Hearsay*)

树丫叉

乡人多以树之丫叉,支为坐凳者。

父命其子求之山中,子持斧去,竟日,徒手归。父责之。子曰:"丫叉尽有,奈都是朝上生的。"

—— 《笑府》

TREE FORKS

The people living on a certain mountain use tree forks for stool legs.

A father sent his son to get one. The son took an axe and went. But at the end of the day he came back empty-handed. When his father scolded him, he answered, "Of course, there are plenty of tree forks there but they all grow upwards."

Xiao Fu (*Treasure-House of Jokes*)

近视眼

有二人短于视,而皆讳言之,喜以目力自多。一日,闻某家于神庙悬扁,乃先侦知其字。是日入庙,一人仰视曰:"美哉,'赫耀声灵'四大字也!"

一人曰:"尚有小字,君未之见,乃'某月日某书'也!"

正共夸诩,旁有一人问曰:"两君会何?"告以所见,其人笑曰:"扁尚未悬,何处有字?"

—— 《笑林新雅》

SHORT-SIGHTEDNESS

Two men were short-sighted, but instead of admitting it, both of them boasted of keen vision.

One day they heard that a tablet was to be hung in a temple. So each of them found out what was written on it beforehand. When the day came, they both went to the temple. Looking up, one said, "Look, aren't the characters 'Brightness and Uprighteousness'?"

"And the smaller ones. There! You can't see them, they say, 'Written by so and so in a certain month, on a certain day'!" said the other.

A passer-by asked what they were looking at. When told, the man laughed. "The tablet hasn't been hoisted up, so how can you see the characters?" he asked.

Xiao Lin Xin Ya(***Selected Jokes***)